GONE WITH
T H E
GRITS

♦ *Diane Pfeifer* ♦

Illustrations by Clark Taylor
Published by Strawberry Patch, Atlanta, Georgia

ISBN: 0-9618306-9-7
Library of Congress Number: 92-090678

Published by: Strawberry Patch
                P.O. Box 52404
                Atlanta, GA 30355-0404
                (404) 261-2197

Editor: Gail Poulton
Design & Composition: Paula Chance, Diva Designs, Atlanta, GA
Back Cover Photography: David Kling
Author Photography: Collin Towers
Food Styling: Paula Chance, Bob Chen (Nakato Restaurant, Atlanta)
Printing: Arcata Graphics, Kingsport, TN
Laplink: Jeff "Mac" Justice

Gone With The Grits is not affiliated with
Mar-GRIT Mitchell's immortal classic.

*This book is dedicated to
my husband Jeff Justice and daughter Jennica Snow, who
were my unfailing taste-testers
through thick and thin
(grits, of course).*

*Most of all, I thank God for giving me such fun ideas and
for making me foolish enough
to do most of them.*

◆ ◆ ◆

*Special thanks to: Amagi's sushi chef in
Hollywood for inspiration,
Gregg Allman for ordering grits,
Chris Verner for grits trivia,
my twin sister Suzanne for support and
Nathalie Dupree and Anne Byrn for grits guidance.*

◆ TABLE OF CONTENTS ◆

Page

Pictured on back cover, clockwise from top left:
Enchilada El-Grito Gringo, page 86; Ranch Dip/Dressing, page 37;
Ila's Cilantro Chutney, page 30; New York Cherry Cheesecake, page 108;
Ah-So Good Vegetarian Nori Rolls, page 82.

GRITS MULTIPLYING

◆ WHY A ◆
GRITS COOKBOOK

*You may wonder what possessed a native Mid-
westerner to write a grits recipe book.*

I admit grits were not exactly a staple of my diet growing up in St. Louis, but my first taste at a Krystal restaurant in Savannah in 1973 hooked me. Shortly thereafter I moved to Atlanta and became a true grits lover. In the ensuing years I wrote country songs for Debby Boone and Roy Clark, toured as a backup singer for Tammy Wynette, recorded wrong number messages for the phone company and wrote a popcorn cookbook, "For Popcorn Lovers Only."

Then, in October '91 I was in Los Angeles to appear on a TV show to demonstrate my popcorn recipes. While dining one night on vegetarian sushi rolls (a Japanese specialty with rice), the chef asked how we prepared sushi rolls in Atlanta. I joked that we used grits instead of rice. While everyone else was laughing I thought, "Why not?... and how about grits as a spicy filling for tacos, in stuffed vegetables, maybe even in breads or cookies or custards — what about a GRITS COOKBOOK?!"

Early the next morning in the hotel coffee shop I was excitedly scribbling recipe ideas when a customer nearby asked the waitress for *GRITS* (in L.A.!). Considering the coincidence I couldn't resist speaking to him and we shared breakfast (sans grits, of course). Who was the customer? The famous Southern blues-rock musician Gregg Allman of the Allman Brothers Band. I *KNEW* I had to write this book.

Before I married my sweet-toothed husband and had our little daughter, I used to dawdle endlessly in the kitchen and never dreamed of making "real" desserts. I share this with you because my cooking style now is quick and easy and includes some slightly sinful Southern sweets. All recipes are vegetarian and in the process of cooking with grits, I discovered some

wonderful ways grits reduce calories in deliciously unique dishes. Most individual recipes also have calorie cutting suggestions.

Not just for breakfast anymore, grits lend a nonfat creaminess to dips and sauces, a sponginess to breads and chewy volume to bar cookies. Cooked with sturdier grains they create exciting and economical meat alternatives for stuffed dishes and casseroles as well as cutlets and burgers. There's even a fun chapter that puts this once laughed-at grain in your favorite foreign dishes.

But the best part will be hearing your family and guests say, "I can't believe it's GRITS!"

TRUE GRITS:

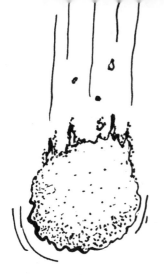

1) Is the word "grits" singular or plural?

A: Definitely singular

B: Positively plural

C: I are not sure either

FACT OR FOLKLORE?

2) Where do grits come from?

A: Grits 'R' Us

B: Hulled dried corn, roughly ground

C: The gritter Atlanta area

3) Who discovered grits?

A: Grits-topher Columbus

B: Marco Polenta

C: Native American Indians

4) Why do only Southerners seem to eat grits?

A: Northerners lack the skill

B: Southerners have great taste

C: It's a tradition

5) What is the difference between grits and hominy?

A: Grits are sung solo, not in 3-part hominy

B: Grits are made from hominy

C: Hominy is made from grits

6) What is a nickname for grits?

A. Junior (or Bubba?)

B. Georgia Ice Cream

C. Stucco

◆ THE BASIC ◆ NITTY GRITTY

There are three kinds of grits eaters and cookers:

1) Those who wait patiently for the creamy rewards of washing, straining, boiling, simmering and stirring old-fashioned stone-ground grits for 40 minutes....

2) Those who need a quick grits fix fast before they miss that important cellular phone call in their car... and...

3) Those who have about 60 seconds to feed the howling toddler and husband clinging to their legs.

Whichever you may be, please follow the appropriate cooking directions given here or on your package. If you need a smaller amount, proportions are about 1 to 4, grits to liquid.

For 1 cup of cooked grits, use about 4 tablespoons grits to 1 cup water and follow cooking directions on grits package. Yield may vary slightly.

Gourmet Grits

◆ BASIC COOKED ◆ STONE-GROUND GRITS

1	cup stone-ground grits
4	cups water
1/2	teaspoon salt
2	tablespoons butter (optional)

Place grits in a large bowl. Cover with cold water and skim off chaff from surface. Stir and skim until all chaff has been removed. Drain grits in a sieve.

In medium saucepan bring water to a boil. Stir in salt then slowly stir in grits. Reduce heat to simmer and cover. Stir frequently until grits are thick and creamy, about 40 minutes.

***Read "Gone With The Wind" again —
you've obviously got the time!***

◆ BASIC COOKED QUICK GRITS ◆

1	cup quick grits
4	cups water
1/2	teaspoon salt
2	tablespoons butter (optional)

In medium saucepan bring water to a boil. Stir in salt then slowly stir in grits. Reduce heat to simmer and cover. Stir frequently until grits are thick and creamy, about 5 minutes.

Remove from heat. Stir in butter if desired.

Hurry up and eat — I think I hear your fax ringing!

◆ BASIC INSTANT GRITS ◆

What are you reading this for? Follow your package directions and cook those grits!! NOW!!

◆ GRITS GROVELINGS ◆ AND HELPFUL HINTS

For really creamy dishes, such as sauces and dips try first blending dry grits in a blender for 5-8 minutes. Then, stir quickly as you pour them into boiling water as they tend to lump if added all at once.

Pots clean easier by letting grits dry in them. They literally "peel" off.

Here are some quick single-serving recipes that turn plain grits into great grits!

Start with one serving of hot, cooked grits.

Then stir in:

1-2	*tablespoons grated cheese OR*
1-2	*tablespoons peanut butter OR*
1-2	*tablespoons preserves OR*
1-2	*tablespoons honey OR*
1-2	*tablespoons maple syrup OR*
1-2	*tablespoons brown sugar and a pinch of cinnamon OR*
1-2	*tablespoons soy bacon bits OR*
1-2	*teaspoons jalapeno peppers or hot sauce*

For variety in texture, try grated apple, raisins, currants, chopped dates or nuts.

For variety in flavor, substitute fruit juices, broths or milk for cooking water.

◆ Basic Fried Grits ◆

1   cup grits
4   cups water
1/2   teaspoon salt
       Butter or margarine

Bring salted water to boil in medium saucepan. Slowly stir in grits. Cover, reduce heat and cook, stirring occasionally until liquid is absorbed according to grits package directions.

Pour into 9x5- or 8x4-inch loaf pan. Cover and refrigerate several hours. Unmold and cut into 1/2-inch slices. Fry on both sides in small amount of butter over medium heat until golden brown.

Serves 6.

Slice and fry cooled leftover grits as well. Great with maple syrup for a sweet treat or with fried onions as a fun substitute for hash browns.

APPEGRITZERS

CREAM CHEESE ROLL-UPS

My cousin Kathy made a similar treat for a Christmas party back home in St. Louis. Next Christmas, they can sample the Southern version.

2	8-ounce packages cream cheese, softened
1	cup cooked grits, cooled (page 12)
2	tablespoons green onion, chopped
1/4	cup black olives, chopped
1/2	teaspoon garlic powder
1/2	teaspoon salt
8	extra-large flour tortillas
	Salsa for dipping

In food processor or mixing bowl, blend or beat cream cheese and grits until creamy. Stir in onion, black olives, garlic powder and salt.

Spread thin layer of mixture on tortilla. Tightly roll up tortilla. Wrap individually in plastic wrap.

Place in refrigerator at least 3 hours or overnight. To serve, cut into 3/4-inch slices.

Makes 45-60 roll-ups.

◆ GRITS CAVIAR ◆

2	*large eggplants*
1	*green pepper*
1	*garlic clove, mashed*
1	*tablespoon fresh parsley*
1	*tablespoon capers*
2	*tablespoons olive oil*
3-4	*tablespoons fresh lemon juice*
4-5	*tablespoons tamari or soy sauce*
	Salt and cayenne to taste
1	*cup cooked grits, hot (page 12)*

Preheat oven to 400°F. Pierce skin of eggplants and pepper with a fork. Line bottom of oven with aluminum foil and place whole eggplants and pepper on oven rack to roast evenly without turning. Pepper will blister in about 25 minutes, eggplants in 50 minutes. Remove when appropriate and let cool enough to handle.

Peel off eggplant and pepper skin and seed the pepper. Scoop out seedy part of eggplant and place in bowl. Place firmer eggplant and pepper pieces in food processor or blender. Add remaining ingredients except hot grits. Blend until combined. Place mixture in bowl with eggplant seeds and stir. Add grits and stir again. Marinate in the refrigerator for at least 2 hours or overnight.

Serves 6-8.

♦ GRITS PATÉ ♦

1	tablespoon olive oil
2/3	cup chopped scallions
1	stalk celery or bok choy, chopped
5	cups sliced mushrooms (about 1-1/2 pounds)
1/2	teaspoon dried basil
1/4	teaspoon dried thyme
1	cup cooked grits (page 12)
1	cup whole wheat bread crumbs
1/2	cup walnuts, chopped
1/4	cup tahini (sesame paste)
3	tablespoons tamari or soy sauce
1/8	teaspoon black pepper
1/8	teaspoon cayenne

Sauté scallions and celery in oil until translucent. Add mushrooms, basil and thyme and cook over low heat until mushrooms are soft. Place sautéed vegetables with rest of ingredients in food processor or blender and blend until smooth.

Oil a medium loaf pan and line it with waxed paper, letting several inches of paper hang over sides of pan. Oil the waxed paper. Spoon in the paté. Fold waxed paper across top and bake for 1-1/2 hours at 400°F.

Paté is done when toothpick inserted in center comes out clean. Let paté cool, then fold back waxed paper on top. Invert paté onto a platter and peel away the waxed paper.

Serve with crudités and crackers.

Serves 6-8.

HERB GRITS-STUFFED MUSHROOMS

8	ounces fresh mushrooms
1	tablespoon butter
1	tablespoon olive oil
2	tablespoons green onion, finely chopped
1	teaspoon fresh parsley or cilantro, chopped
1-2	cloves garlic, minced
1	teaspoon salt
	Pepper to taste
1	cup cooked grits, warm (page 12)

Wash mushrooms. Remove and save stems. Put caps in shallow baking dish. Heat butter and oil in medium pan. Finely chop stems and sauté with onion until soft.

Add parsley, garlic, salt and pepper. Cook for 1 minute. Stir in grits to make a stiff mixture. Stuff each cap and bake at 350°F for 15 minutes.

Serves 6-8.

My little daughter ate half the filling before I could stuff the mushrooms.

◆

◆ SPINACH BALLS ◆

2	*packages frozen chopped spinach*
1	*large yellow onion, finely chopped*
3/4	*cup butter or margarine, melted*
4	*eggs, beaten*
1/2	*cup Parmesan cheese*
1/2	*teaspoon garlic powder*
1/2	*teaspoon salt*
1	*cup cooked grits (page 12)*
2	*cups dry stuffing mix*

Cook and drain spinach and place in large mixing bowl. Add remaining ingredients, mixing thoroughly with hands. Refrigerate until chilled. Shape into 1-inch balls. Place on greased cookie sheet. Bake at 350°F for 20-25 minutes. Can be frozen before being baked.

Serves 6-8.

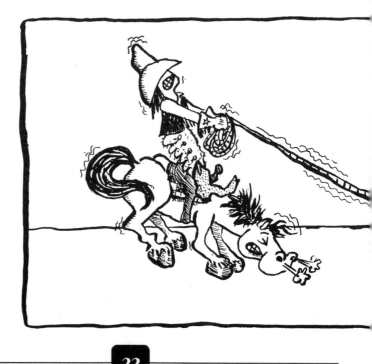

◆ TANGY RANCH SQUARES ◆

1	cup grits
4	cups water
1	teaspoon salt
2	1-ounce envelopes dry ranch dressing mix, divided
1	tablespoon flour
	Butter or oil for frying

Bring salted water to boil in medium saucepan. Slowly stir in grits. Cover, reduce heat and cook, stirring occasionally until liquid is absorbed according to grits package directions. Reserve 3 tablespoons ranch dressing mix. Add remaining dressing mix to hot grits and stir thoroughly.

Spread in 9x13-inch pan and let cool until firm. Cut into 2-inch squares. Combine flour and remaining dressing mix in medium bowl. Coat grits squares in breading mixture until all sides are well-coated. Heat butter or oil in large skillet. Fry grits until crispy.

Serves 6-8.

◆ NOT-CHO GRITS ◆

1	cup grits
4	cups water
1	teaspoon salt
1-1/2	cups grated cheddar cheese
1/2	teaspoon cumin
1/4	teaspoon oregano
1/2	teaspoon chili powder
1/2	teaspoon garlic powder
1/2	teaspoon onion powder
	Cayenne pepper to taste
	Tortilla chips
	Prepared bean dip
	Prepared guacamole dip
	Sour cream
	Jalapeno peppers, seeded and thinly sliced

Bring salted water to boil in medium saucepan. Slowly stir in grits. Cover, reduce heat and cook, stirring occasionally until liquid is absorbed according to grits package directions. Stir in cheese and spices, mixing thoroughly. If smoother texture is desired, blend mixture in food processor or blender until creamy.

Spread tortilla chips with small amount of bean dip and cheese grits mixture. If softer nacho is desired, microwave or broil until softened. Top with guacamole dip and sour cream. Garnish liberally with sliced jalapenos. Makes a great nacho cheese dip, too.

Calorie cutter: *Use lowfat cheese and sour cream.*

Vegetarians: Use bean dip with no lard.

Shortcut: Substitute taco seasoning mix to taste for spices.

Serves 6-8.

◆ DEVILED EGGS ◆

12	*hard-boiled eggs, peeled*
1/4	*cup cooked grits (page 12)*
2-3	*tablespoons mayonnaise*
1	*tablespoon Dijon mustard*
1/2	*teaspoon black pepper*
1/2	*teaspoon paprika*
2	*tablespoons sweet relish*
1	*tablespoon chopped cilantro (optional)*
2	*tablespoons celery, finely minced*
2	*tablespoons green onion, finely sliced*
1	*tablespoon red bell pepper, finely minced*

Slice eggs in half lengthways. Gently scoop out yolks. Place yolks, grits, mayonnaise, mustard, black pepper and paprika in mixing bowl or food processor. Blend thoroughly until creamy. Stir in remaining ingredients.

With rounded teaspoon, stuff egg whites with filling. Sprinkle tops with paprika. Save extra filling for pita sandwiches.

Makes 24 deviled eggs.

CRISPY PARMESAN SQUARES

I waited 37 years to get married and somehow landed a guy who doesn't like Parmesan cheese. But he has a great sense of humor and he can reach my top kitchen shelves — both very important in a mate.

4	cups water
1	cup grits
1/2	teaspoon salt
1-1/2	cups Parmesan cheese
2	tablespoons flour
1/2	teaspoon seasoning salt
1/2	teaspoon pepper
	Butter or oil for frying

Bring salted water to boil in medium saucepan. Slowly stir in grits. Cover, reduce heat and cook, stirring occasionally until liquid is absorbed according to grits package directions. Stir in 1 cup Parmesan cheese.

Spread in 9x13-inch pan and let cool until firm. Cut into 2-inch squares.

Combine flour, seasoning salt, pepper and remaining Parmesan cheese in medium bowl. Coat grits squares in breading mixture, turning until all sides are well-coated.

Melt butter in large skillet. Fry grits until crispy on both sides.

Serves 6-8.

DIPS AND
◆ DRESSINGS ◆

◆ DA GRITCI PESTO SAUCE ◆

1   cup cooked grits, warm (page 12)
1/4   cup olive oil
1   small bunch fresh basil
2   cloves garlic
1/2   cup grated Parmesan cheese
1/4   cup pine nuts, toasted
      Salt to taste

Place all ingredients in food processor or blender and blend until creamy. Thin with small amount of water as needed. Serve warm over linguine or your favorite pasta.

Calorie cutter: *Forget it.*

Makes about 2 cups.

BIT O' GRITS

COOKING
WEIGHTS AND MEASURES

MESS O' GRITS

SPICY SZECHUAN PEANUT SAUCE

1	cup cooked grits (page 12)
2	tablespoons sesame oil
3	tablespoons sesame paste
2	tablespoons peanut butter
2	tablespoons tamari or soy sauce
1-2	cloves garlic, pressed
1/4	teaspoon fresh ginger root, minced
1/8	teaspoon cayenne pepper, or to taste
3	teaspoons brown sugar
2	teaspoons rice vinegar
3	tablespoons green onion tops, thinly sliced

Adapted from a spicy noodle dish served at my favorite Atlanta restaurant, Grand China.

In food processor or blender blend all ingredients except 1 tablespoon green onions. Blend until creamy. Thin with small amount of water if too thick.

Toss over cold cooked Chinese noodles and garnish with green onions as a dinner starter. Makes a unique party dip as well.

Makes 1-1/2 cups.

ILA'S CILANTRO CHUTNEY

◆

One taste of this chutney magically takes my husband and me back to our inspiring trips to South India. Our dear friend Ila brings this fragrant, fiery condiment to potluck and I can't wait to share my grits version next time!

◆

3	large cloves garlic
1	tablespoon ginger root, grated
1/2-1	teaspoon hot green chilies, minced*
1	heaping teaspoon sugar
3	tablespoons cashews
	Juice of 2-3 lemons
1	teaspoon powdered caraway powder
1/2	cups cooked grits (page 12)
	Salt to taste
2	bunches cilantro leaves, some stems

Place all ingredients except cilantro in food processor and blend until smooth. Slowly add handfuls of cilantro and continue chopping and blending until chutney is smooth. Add small amounts of any ingredient until desired flavor is achieved.

Let sit 2 hours or overnight for flavor enhancement.

*Ila's version calls for a tablespoon of hot green chilies, but for our Western palate I find it best to start with a teaspoon or less and add more as needed.

Serve with rice or — why not — grits!

Makes a great dip for veggies, too!

Makes 2-3 cups.

*G*rits add creamy volume to dips with no
extra fat. In sour cream recipes,
substitute light or regular cream cheese to create
quick, delicious sandwich spreads.

◆ ◆ ◆ ◆

HUMMUS DIP

1	cup cooked grits (page 12)
4-5	tablespoons fresh lemon juice
1/2	cup tahini
3	garlic cloves, pressed
1	teaspoon salt
	Cayenne powder to taste
1	15-ounce can garbanzo beans, drained and reserved
1/4	cup chopped parsley

In blender or food processor, blend grits, lemon juice, tahini,
garlic, salt, cayenne and 1/4 cup bean liquid until smooth. Add
garbanzo beans, blending to a rough consistency—not too smooth.
Stir in parsley.

Makes 2-3 cups.

BABA GANOUSH DIP

Lemon and sesame paste give this eggplant dip a wonderfully unique flavor and the grits add creaminess with no fat.

1	medium eggplant
1	cup cooked grits (page 12)
1/2	cup tahini (sesame paste)
3-4	garlic cloves, mashed with 1 teaspoon salt
4	tablespoons fresh lemon juice
1/2	teaspoon cumin (optional)
	Finely chopped parsley, cayenne or paprika

Place eggplant in baking dish. Broil 4 inches from flame for 20 minutes. Turn occasionally and puncture skin to let steam escape. Remove and let cool enough to handle. Peel off skin.

In blender or food processor, blend grits, tahini, garlic-salt mixture and lemon juice until smooth. Add eggplant and spices, if desired and blend again. Garnish with parsley or cayenne and paprika.

Makes about 3 cups.

◆ GARDEN ◆
VEGETA-BOWL DIP

1	cup cooked grits, cooled (page 12)
1/2	cup sour cream
1/2	cup mayonnaise
1	teaspoon lemon pepper
1	teaspoon garlic powder
1	teaspoon onion powder
1/4	teaspoon paprika
2	tablespoons finely diced carrot
1	tablespoon finely diced green pepper
1	tablespoon finely diced red pepper
2	tablespoons finely diced celery
2	teaspoons parsley flakes
	Salt and pepper to taste

Place grits, sour cream and mayonnaise in food processor. Blend until creamy, about 6 minutes. Stir in remaining ingredients. Chill for a few hours. Stir thoroughly before serving.

Calorie cutter: *Use light sour cream and mayonnaise.*

Shortcut: Use 3-4 tablespoons dry vegetable soup mix for dry ingredients.

Makes about 2-1/2 cups.

◆ CREAMY ONION DIP ◆

1	cup cooked grits, cooled (page 12)
1/2	cup sour cream
1	8-ounce package cream cheese, softened
1	1-ounce envelope onion soup mix

Place grits, sour cream and cream cheese in food processor or blender. Blend until creamy, about 6 minutes. Add remaining sour cream and soup mix. Blend for 2 more minutes. Chill for a few hours. Stir thoroughly before serving.

Calorie cutter: *Use light sour cream and cream cheese.*

Vegetarians: Use onion soup mix without beef stock.

Makes about 2-1/2 cups.

◆ DILL GRITS DIP ◆

1	cup cooked grits, cooled (page 12)
1	cup sour cream
2-3	tablespoons dried or fresh minced dillweed
1/2	teaspoon garlic powder
1/2	teaspoon salt

Place grits and sour cream in food processor. Blend until creamy, about 6 minutes. Blend in remaining ingredients. Chill for a few hours to enhance flavor. Stir thoroughly before serving.

Calorie cutter: *Use light sour cream.*

Makes about 2 cups.

◆ TACO DIP ◆

1	cup cooked grits, cooled (page 12)
1	cup sour cream
1/2-1	tablespoon dry taco mix seasoning

Place grits and sour cream in food processor or blender. Blend until creamy, about 6 minutes. Add taco mix to taste and blend again. Chill for a few hours to enhance flavor and thicken mixture. Stir thoroughly before serving.

Calorie cutter: *Use light sour cream.*

Makes about 2 cups.

SOUR CREAM 'N' CHIVES DIP

I took this to a Christmas party and nobody could guess the secret ingredient—except the fifty or so people I told about my grits cookbook-in-progress.

1   cup cooked grits, cooled (page 12)
1   cup sour cream
1   teaspoon garlic powder
1   teaspoon onion powder
3   tablespoons chopped fresh chives
1/2   teaspoon salt

Place grits and sour cream in food processor or blender. Blend until creamy, about 6 minutes. Add garlic and onion powder and blend again. Stir in chives. Chill for a few hours to enhance flavor and thicken mixture. Stir thoroughly before serving.

Calorie cutter: *Use light sour cream.*

Makes about 2 cups.

BA-CORN HORSERADISH

1   cup cooked grits, cooled (page 12)
1   cup sour cream
1-1/2   tablespoons prepared horseradish
2   tablespoons soy bacon bits

Place grits and sour cream in food processor or blender. Blend until creamy, about 6 minutes. Stir in horseradish to taste and soy bacon bits. Chill a few hours to enhance flavor and thicken mixture. Stir thoroughly before serving.

Calorie cutter: *Use light sour cream.*

Makes about 2 cups.

◆ CREAMY CAESAR SALAD ◆ DRESSING

1/2	cup cooked grits (page 12)
3	cloves garlic
	Juice of 1 lemon
1/4	cup olive oil
1/2	teaspoon coarsely ground black pepper
1	egg yolk
1/4	teaspoon Worcestershire sauce
1/2	cup grated Parmesan cheese
1	teaspoon salt or to taste
1/2-1	cup water

In food processor or blender, blend all ingredients until creamy. Thin to desired consistency with water.

Calorie cutter: *Use 2 tablespoons olive oil.*

Vegetarians: Use Worcestershire sauce without anchovies. Yes, they are little fishies.

Makes 2-3 cups.

◆ RANCH DIP/DRESSING ◆

1	cup cooked grits, cooled (page 12)
3/4	cup sour cream
1/4	cup mayonnaise
1	envelope dry ranch dressing mix

Place grits and sour cream in food processor or blender. Blend until creamy, about 6 minutes. Add mayonnaise and dressing mix and blend again. Chill for a few hours. Stir thoroughly before serving. If necessary, thin with a little water for dressing.

Calorie cutter: *Use light sour cream and mayonnaise.*

Makes about 2 cups.

◆ LEMON TAHINI DRESSING ◆

1	cup tahini (sesame paste)
1	cup cooked grits, cooled (page 12)
1/2	cup lemon juice
1/4	cup olive oil
2-3	tablespoons tamari or soy sauce
1/2	teaspoon black pepper
1/4	cup chopped scallions
1-2	large cloves garlic, pressed
	Dash cayenne, turmeric and salt, if needed
	Water

In food processor or blender, blend all ingredients together until smooth. Let sit at least an hour or overnight to let flavors blend and mixture thicken. Thin with a little water, if needed.

Variation: Blend in 1/2 medium green or red bell pepper for color and flavor variety.

Makes about 2-1/2 cups.

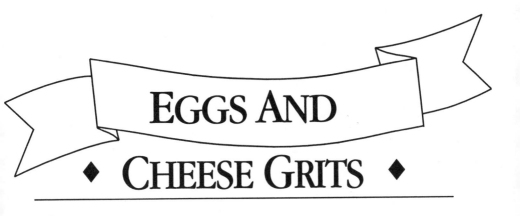

EGGS AND

◆ CHEESE GRITS ◆

◆ CHEESE BLINTZES ◆

Filling:

1	cup cooked grits (page 12)
1	cup ricotta cheese
1	egg yolk
2	tablespoons sugar

Crepes:

1	recipe Swedish Crepes (below)

Toppings:

Sour cream, whipped cream,
fresh fruit, preserves, honey, yogurt

Combine filling ingredients in bowl. Fill crepes and roll up. Arrange in baking dish. Bake 15-20 minutes at 350°F. Top with sour cream and/or preserves or other suggested toppings.

Serves 6.

◆ SWEDISH CREPES ◆

2-1/2	cups milk
2-1/4	cups all-purpose flour
	Pinch salt
2	eggs
	Butter or oil for frying

In large mixing bowl or blender, blend or beat milk and flour together until smooth. Add salt and eggs and beat well. Let stand for an hour.

Heat a little butter or oil in heavy-bottomed 7-inch skillet, preferably a crepe pan. Tip out excess butter. When pan is very hot, add 2 tablespoons batter. Tilt pan so batter covers bottom. Cook until crepe begins to brown on underside then turn over and cook other side.

Continue making crepes, keeping them warm until all batter is used.

Makes 9 small crepes.

◆ CHEESE BLINTZ SOUFFLÉ ◆

1	recipe Cheese Blintzes, unbaked (page 40)
1/4	cup butter or margarine, melted
4	eggs
1/2	cup sugar
1/2	cup orange juice
1/2	teaspoon vanilla
1-1/2	cups sour cream

Pour butter into 9x13-inch baking dish. Arrange blintzes in dish. Beat eggs, sugar, orange juice and vanilla. Add sour cream and mix well. Pour over blintzes. Bake uncovered for 45 minutes at 350°F.

Serves 6.

◆ GRIT-TLE CAKES ◆

1	egg, well beaten
1/3	cup milk
2	teaspoons grated onion
2	cups cooked grits (page 12)
1/2	teaspoon garlic powder
2	cups water
1/4	cup all-purpose flour
1-1/2	teaspoons baking powder
1	teaspoon sugar or honey
	Salt and pepper to taste
	Sour cream or plain yogurt

Combine egg with milk and onion. Stir in grits. Combine remaining ingredients. Add to grits mixture. Mix slightly. Drop by tablespoons onto hot griddle. Cook until brown on each side. Serve with applesauce and/or sour cream or plain yogurt.

Calorie cutter: *Use light sour cream or lowfat yogurt.*

Serves 6.

ZUCCHINI POTATO PANCAKES

My 3-year-
old devoured
these –
topped with
catsup
(groan)!

1	cup cooked grits, warm (page 12)
3	eggs
1	tablespoon flour
1	tablespoon tamari or soy sauce
1	teaspoon salt
1/2	teaspoon black pepper
1/2	teaspoon garlic powder
1/2	cup Parmesan cheese
2	large zucchini, grated
2	large potatoes, grated
1/2	small onion, minced
	Oil for frying

Toppings:
Sour cream or plain yogurt
and/or applesauce

In large mixing bowl, beat grits and eggs. Stir in remaining ingredients. Heat 1 tablespoon oil in skillet or large pan over medium heat. Drop 2 tablespoons batter per pancake, cooking until both sides are crispy and golden. Serve with suggested toppings.

Calorie cutter: *Use light sour cream or lowfat yogurt.*

Serves 6.

◆ GRITS AU GRATIN ◆

1	cup grits
4	cups water
1-1/2	teaspoons salt
2	eggs
1-1/2	cups sharp cheddar cheese, grated
1/3	cup butter or margarine
1-2	cloves garlic, crushed
	Dash of hot sauce

Preheat oven to 350°F. Bring salted water to boil in medium saucepan. Slowly stir in grits. Cover, reduce heat and cook, stirring occasionally until liquid is absorbed according to grits package directions. Remove from heat.

Whisk eggs slightly, then stir in small amount of grits to warm them. Beat egg mixture into grits. Stir in remaining ingredients, mixing well. Pour grits mixture into greased 1-1/2-quart casserole. Bake for 30-45 minutes depending on depth of dish.

Calorie cutter: *Use lowfat cheese and diet margarine.*

Variations: Add other omelet items such as soy bacon bits, minced onion, green pepper flakes, chopped mushrooms or other favorites.

Serves 6.

MCBACON CHEESE GRITS CASSEROLE

Shortcut:
Forget the eggs, don't bake it and serve right from the pan.

1	cup grits
4	cups water
1	teaspoon salt
1	cup sharp cheddar cheese, grated
2	tablespoons butter
1	teaspoon liquid or dry smoke seasoning
2	tablespoons tamari or soy sauce
1/4	cup soy bacon bits
1	teaspoon pepper
2	eggs, beaten
	Dash hot sauce (optional)

Bring salted water to boil in medium saucepan. Slowly stir in grits. Cover, reduce heat and cook, stirring occasionally until liquid is absorbed according to grits package directions.

Stir in remaining ingredients and place in greased 2-quart casserole. Bake at 350°F for 1 hour.

Calorie cutter: *Use diet margarine and lowfat cheese.*

Serves 6.

◆ CHEESE GRITS BURRITO ◆

1	cup grits
4	cups water
1	teaspoon salt
1	cup sharp cheddar cheese, grated
2	tablespoons butter
3	eggs, beaten
1-2	cloves garlic, crushed
1	teaspoon pepper
	Cayenne pepper to taste
10-12	flour tortillas
	Salsa

Bring salted water to boil in medium saucepan. Slowly stir in grits. Cover, reduce heat and cook, stirring occasionally until liquid is absorbed according to grits package directions.

Stir in cheese, butter, eggs, garlic and peppers. Heat through enough to cook eggs.

Heat tortillas one at a time for 10 seconds on each side in hot skillet. Fill center with 1/2 cup grits mixture. Top with small amount of salsa. Fold bottom of tortilla up towards center, then fold sides towards center.

Serves 6.

◆ SWISS CHEESE PIE ◆

2   *eggs*
1   *cup cooked grits, warm (page 12)*
1/2   *cup evaporated milk*
4   *cups Swiss cheese, grated*
1   *tablespoon butter or margarine*
       Salt and pepper to taste
       Dash paprika or nutmeg, optional
1   *9-inch unbaked pie crust (page 96)*

Preheat oven to 350°F. In mixing bowl, beat eggs, grits, evaporated milk, salt and pepper. Fill unbaked pie crust with grated cheese and pour grits mixture over it. Dot with butter and sprinkle with paprika or nutmeg. Bake for 55-65 minutes until golden, crisp and set in center.

Vegetarians: If using a premade pie crust, use one made without lard.

Variation: Add 1/4 cup minced onion, sautéed sliced mushrooms or pimientos to batter. Also good baked without the crust!

Serves 6.

SIDE GRITS

GRITS RICE PILAF

3	tablespoons butter or margarine
1	cup brown or white rice
1/2	cup grits
2-1/2	tablespoons powdered vegetable or chicken-flavored bouillon
1	tablespoon dried parsley flakes
	Pepper to taste
5-6	cups water
1/2	cup toasted pine nuts

Melt butter in medium saucepan. Add rice and grits. Stir to coat for 1 minute. Stir in bouillon, parsley flakes, pepper and 5 cups water. Bring water to boil.

Reduce heat to simmer and cover. Determine length of cooking according to rice type or package directions. Check grains occasionally and add more water if necessary. When grains are done, place in serving bowl and stir in pine nuts.

Vegetarians: Use a vegetarian chicken-flavored substitute available at most health food stores.

Serves 6.

◆

Super for stuffing squash, eggplant, artichokes and other vegetables.

◆

❖ HONEY-STUFFED ACORN SQUASH ❖

3	acorn squash, halved, seeds removed

Filling:

1	cup cooked grits, warm (page 12)
2/3	cup honey
3	tablespoons butter or margarine, melted
1/2	teaspoon cinnamon
1/4	cup chopped nuts
1/4	cup raisins

Preheat oven to 350°F. Place squash, cut side down, in shallow pan of water. Bake for 30-45 minutes until tender. (Or bake ahead and refrigerate.) Combine filling ingredients. Fill squash cavities and place, cut side up in a baking dish. Bake for 15-20 minutes more, until hot.

Serves 6.

❖ CHEESE-STUFFED ACORN SQUASH ❖

3	acorn squash, halved, seeds removed
1	cup cooked grits, warm (page 12)
1/2	cup grated cheddar cheese
1/4	cup chopped nuts
6	tablespoons butter or margarine

Preheat oven to 350°F. Place squash, cut side down, in shallow pan of water. Bake for 30-45 minutes until tender. (Or bake ahead and refrigerate.) Combine grits, cheese and nuts. Fill each squash cavity with 1 tablespoon butter then fill to top with cheese grits mixture. Place cut side up in a baking dish.

Bake for 10-15 minutes more, until hot.

Serves 6.

GRITS-TOPHER COLUMBUS HERB GRITS

Serve with fresh vegetables that have been stir-fried in olive oil with a dash of basil, oregano and/or marjoram. Share your discovery with friends.

1	cup grits
4	cups water
1-1/2	teaspoons salt
2	tablespoons butter or margarine
1	tablespoon olive oil
1/2	teaspoon oregano
1/2	teaspoon basil
1/2	teaspoon marjoram
1	teaspoon garlic powder
1	teaspoon onion powder
1/2	cup grated Parmesan cheese

Bring salted water to boil in medium saucepan. Slowly stir in grits. Cover, reduce heat and cook, stirring occasionally until liquid is absorbed according to grits package directions. Stir in butter, oil, oregano, basil, marjoram, garlic powder and onion powder. Sprinkle with Parmesan cheese.

Variation: Pour mixture into 9x13-inch pan and chill 4 hours or overnight. Cut into 2-inch squares.

Heat small amount of butter in skillet. Fry grits until golden and crispy on both sides. Serve lightly topped with warmed marinara sauce and sprinkle of Parmesan cheese.

Calorie cutter: *Skip the olive oil and use diet margarine.*

Serves 6.

◆ THE GRITFATHER ◆

1	cup grits
4	cups water
1	teaspoon salt
2	tablespoons olive oil
1	tablespoon butter or margarine
2-3	cloves garlic, pressed
1/2	cup grated Parmesan cheese

Bring salted water to boil in medium saucepan. Slowly stir in grits. Cover, reduce heat and cook, stirring occasionally until liquid is absorbed according to grits package directions. Melt butter and olive oil in small pan over low heat. Sauté garlic briefly. Stir into grits. Add Parmesan cheese and mix again.

Calorie cutter: *Use 2 tablespoons diet margarine instead of butter and olive oil. Decrease Parmesan cheese by 1/2 cup.*

Shortcut: Substitute 1 tablespoon prepared garlic butter for garlic and butter.

Serves 6.

◆ CILANTRO TABOULI SALAD ◆

2	cups boiling water
1/2	teaspoon salt
1	cup bulghur (cracked) wheat
1	cup cooked grits, warm (page 12)
1	cup minced cilantro
1/2	cup minced green onion tops
1/4	cup olive oil
	Juice of 1-2 lemons
	Salt and pepper to taste

Pour boiling salted water over bulghur in medium bowl. Let sit for 30 minutes to absorb water. Stir in warm grits and mix. Toss all other ingredients into the grain mixture. Add salt and pepper to taste. Chill to enhance flavor. Serve on lettuce as salad.

Serves 6.

RICOTTA DUMPLINGS

Vegetarians:

Use a vegetarian chicken-flavored substitute available at most health food stores.

6-8	*cups vegetable or chicken-flavored broth*
1/2	*cup grated Parmesan cheese*
1/2	*cup ricotta cheese*
1	*cup cooked grits, cooled (page 12)*
1/2	*cup all-purpose flour*
1	*large egg, lightly beaten*
2	*tablespoons fresh basil, parsley or cilantro, minced*
	Green onion tops, thinly sliced

Heat broth until simmering in large pot. In medium bowl, stir the Parmesan, ricotta, grits, flour, egg, and herb of choice just until smooth. Scoop up about 1 tablespoon mixture with rounded spoon and with second spoon, smooth top into a dumpling. Drop into simmering soup and repeat until all dumplings are formed.

Simmer until dumplings are cooked through, about 6 minutes. Serve in bowl with broth and top with green onion.

Serves 6.

◆ CAJUN CORN ◆

1	cup grits
4	cups water
1-1/2	teaspoons salt
3	tablespoons butter or margarine
1	teaspoon garlic powder
1	teaspoon onion powder
2	teaspoons paprika
1/4	teaspoon ground white pepper or to taste
1/2	teaspoon ground black pepper
1/2	teaspoon filé powder (optional)
	Bottled hot sauce, optional

Bring salted water to boil in medium saucepan. Slowly stir in grits. Cover, reduce heat and cook, stirring occasionally until liquid is absorbed according to grits package directions. Add butter, garlic and spices. Serve with hot sauce.

Serves 6.

Goodness gracious,

GRIT BOWLS O' FIRE!

CREOLE
◆ BEANS & GRITS ◆

3	tablespoons vegetable oil
2	cups chopped onions
5	garlic cloves, minced or pressed
1	green pepper, chopped
1	celery stalk, diced
1	tablespoon parsley, chopped
1/3	cup tomato paste
1/4	cup red wine or vegetable broth
1	teaspoon apple cider vinegar
1-1/2	teaspoons brown sugar
	Salt and cayenne pepper to taste
1/2	teaspoon dried oregano
1/8	teaspoon ground allspice
4	cups cooked red beans, drained

Grits:

4	cups water
1	teaspoon salt
1	cup grits
1/8	teaspoon cayenne pepper
1/8	teaspoon ground allspice
2	tablespoons butter or margarine
	Salsa
	Sour cream

Sauté the onions and garlic in oil on medium heat until onions are translucent. Add green pepper, celery and parsley and cook several minutes longer. Stir occasionally, sautéing until vegetables are tender.

Whisk together the tomato paste, wine or broth, vinegar, sugar, spices and herbs. Add mixture to sautéed vegetables. In large pot, combine drained beans and sautéed vegetable mixture, stirring to mix. Cover and simmer for 30 minutes, stirring frequently.

In medium saucepan, bring salted water to boil. Slowly stir in grits, cayenne, allspice and butter. Cover, reduce heat and cook, stirring occasionally until liquid is absorbed according to grits package directions. When both beans and grits are done, prepare each serving with a layer of grits, then beans. Top with spoonful of salsa and sour cream.

Serves 6.

BLACKENED CAJUN SQUARES

1	*cup grits*
4	*cups water*
1	*teaspoon salt*
6	*tablespoons flour*
2	*teaspoons salt*
2	*teaspoons paprika*
1/2	*teaspoon ground white pepper*
1/2	*teaspoon ground black pepper*
1/2	*teaspoon filé powder (optional)*
	Butter or margarine for frying

Bring salted water to boil in medium saucepan. Slowly stir in grits. Cover, reduce heat and cook, stirring occasionally until liquid is absorbed according to grits package directions.

Pour into 9x13-inch pan. Let cool until firm, at least four hours or overnight. Cut into 2-inch squares.

Mix remaining breading ingredients and place on large plate. Coat grits in mixture on all sides. Melt butter in large skillet and fry squares until dark on each side.

Variation: If you're really brave, prepare a batch of "Cajun Corn" (page 53) and pour into loaf pan. Proceed as above. A double-alarm fire!

Serves 6.

◆

Be careful when frying cooled grits – they tend to "spit" a little.

◆

◆ GEORGIA FRENCH FRIES ◆

1	*cup grits*
4	*cups water*
1	*teaspoon salt*
6	*tablespoons flour*
1	*teaspoon salt*
1/2	*teaspoon pepper*
1/2	*teaspoon lemon pepper*
1/2	*teaspoon seasoning salt*
1	*teaspoon paprika*
	Butter or oil for frying

Bring salted water to boil in medium saucepan. Slowly stir in grits. Cover, reduce heat and cook, stirring occasionally until liquid is absorbed according to grits package directions. Spread in 9x13-inch pan and let cool until firm.

Cut into French fry-size pieces. Combine flour, salt, pepper, lemon pepper, seasoning salt and paprika in medium bowl. Coat grits strips in breading mixture on all sides. Melt butter in large skillet. Fry grits until crispy on all sides.

Shortcut: Substitute packaged flour-type coating mix for breading ingredients.

Serves 6.

MAIN

◆ DISHES ◆

QUICK NO-CRUST SPINACH QUICHE

Options:
1/4 cup chopped pimientos, chopped red bell peppers, soy bacon bits, diced steamed vegetables

1	10-ounce package frozen chopped spinach, cooked and drained
	OR
2/3	cup cooked fresh spinach, drained
1	tablespoon butter or margarine
1	medium onion, diced
4	eggs
1	13-ounce can evaporated milk
	Salt and pepper to taste
	Dash nutmeg (optional)
1	cup cooked grits, warm (page 12)
1/2	pound grated Swiss cheese
1/2	cup grated Parmesan cheese

In frying pan, sauté drained spinach, butter and onion. Set aside. In large mixing bowl or food processor, beat or blend eggs, milk, salt, pepper, optional nutmeg and grits until creamy. Stir in spinach mixture, Swiss cheese, half the Parmesan cheese and any optional ingredients.

Pour mixture into 10-inch quiche dish. Sprinkle the remaining Parmesan cheese on top. Bake at 350°F for 40-45 minutes.

Calorie cutters: *Use evaporated skim milk and lowfat Swiss cheese. Skip the 1/4 cup Parmesan cheese topping.*

Serves 6.

◆ CHEESY SPINACH MUSHROOM ◆ CASSEROLE

1	package frozen chopped spinach
1	cup grits
3-4	cups water
1	teaspoon salt
1	egg, beaten
1	can cream of mushroom soup
1	cup cheddar cheese, grated
1	cup buttered bread crumbs or cracker crumbs

Preheat oven to 350°F. Cook spinach and drain liquid into measuring cup. Reserve spinach for later use. Add enough water to spinach liquid to make 4 cups. Place liquid and salt in medium saucepan and bring to boil. Stir in grits slowly. Cover, reduce heat and cook, stirring occasionally until liquid is absorbed according to grits package directions.

Stir in egg, soup, cheese and spinach. Place in 2-quart casserole. Bake for 10-15 minutes. Top with buttered crumbs and bake for 5 more minutes.

Serves 6.

PIMIENTO CHEESE GRITS

This is a quick "what's left in the kitchen" recipe that makes a hearty, delicious dinner. Try experimenting with other cream soups and cheeses for variety.

1	cup grits
4	cups water
1/2	teaspoon salt
1	can cream of mushroom soup
2	cups cheddar cheese, grated
1	4-ounce jar pimientos, chopped
	Salt and pepper to taste
	Whole pimientos sliced for garnish (optional)

Bring salted water to boil in medium saucepan. Slowly stir in grits. Cover, reduce heat and cook, stirring occasionally until liquid is absorbed according to grits package directions.

Stir in soup, 1-1/2 cups cheese, pimientos and pepper until thoroughly mixed. Heat through. Place in large casserole. Sprinkle top with remaining cheese and allow to melt. Garnish with sliced pimientos if desired.

Serves 6.

◆ Broccoli Mushroom Pie ◆

2	cups milk
3	tablespoons uncooked grits
3	tablespoons butter or margarine, divided
1	teaspoon salt
3	eggs
	Pepper to taste
1	cup broccoli flowerets, chopped
1-1/2	cups fresh mushrooms, sliced
2	tablespoons pimientos or red bell peppers, chopped
1	green onion, minced
	Dash nutmeg or cayenne
1	tablespoon flour
1	9-inch pie crust, prebaked 3-4 minutes (page 96)

Bring milk, grits, 1 tablespoon butter and salt to simmer over low heat in medium saucepan. Cook, stirring frequently until grits thicken and get soft, about 8-10 minutes. Set aside.

Beat eggs and pepper until frothy. Stir into grits mixture. Meanwhile, sauté broccoli, mushrooms, pimientos and green onions in remaining butter in small skillet until heated through. Sprinkle with flour and stir thoroughly.

Combine vegetable mixture and grits mixture, stirring thoroughly. Pour into pie crust. Bake in 325°F oven until top is slightly browned, 40-45 minutes.

Substitute other sautéed or even leftover vegetables in the same quantities for a last-minute meal.

Vegetarians: If using a premade pie crust, use one without lard.

Makes 1 pie.

◆ SHEPHERD'S POT PIE ◆

Crust:

1	19-ounce can garbanzo beans, liquid reserved
1	cup cooked grits, warm (page 12)
1	tablespoon olive oil
1	teaspoon salt
1/4	teaspoon pepper

Filling:

1	medium yellow onion, diced
1	clove garlic, minced
1	cup sliced mushrooms
2	tablespoons butter or margarine
1	packet vegetable bouillon
1	bay leaf
	Salt and pepper to taste
2	cups chopped vegetables (cooked or uncooked)
1	tablespoon unbleached white flour
1/4	cup water
1/2	cup cheddar cheese, grated

In food processor or blender, blend crust ingredients with 1/4 cup bean liquid until creamy and fluffy enough to spread. If mixture gets too thick, blend with small amount of bean liquid.

Sauté onion, garlic and mushrooms in butter over low heat until onion is soft. Add vegetable bouillon, remaining bean liquid, bay leaf, salt and pepper and bring to simmer. Stir in chopped vegetables.

Dissolve flour in 1/4 cup water. Pour into vegetable mixture and stir until slightly thickened. Cook vegetables for 5 more minutes. Remove bay leaf. Pour vegetable mixture into 2-quart casserole. Spread grits crust mixture over top, sealing edges.

Bake at 325°F for 15-20 minutes until top is golden. Remove and sprinkle with cheese. Bake 5 more minutes.

Serves 6-8.

◆ Spinach Lasagna ◆

1	cup grits
4	cups water
1	teaspoon salt
1-1/2	cups Parmesan cheese
1	cup ricotta cheese
1	cup cottage cheese
1	egg
1	10-ounce package frozen spinach, cooked and drained
1	teaspoon garlic powder
1/2	teaspoon black pepper
4	cups spaghetti sauce
3	cups mozzarella cheese, grated

Bring salted water to boil in medium saucepan. Slowly stir in grits. Cover, reduce heat and cook, stirring occasionally until liquid is absorbed according to grits package directions. Pour grits into 9x5-inch pan and let cool until firm. Slice cooled grits into 1/2-inch slices and set aside.

In large bowl, mix together 1/2 cup Parmesan cheese, ricotta cheese, cottage cheese, egg, spinach, garlic powder and pepper. Preheat oven to 325°F.

Grease a 2-quart casserole. Place a thin layer of sauce on bottom. Next place a layer of grits slices. Cover grits with 1/2 of the spinach mixture. Spoon on thin layer of tomato sauce. Sprinkle on 1 cup grated mozzarella and 1/2 cup Parmesan cheese. Repeat layers with remaining ingredients.

Bake for 25-30 minutes.

Serves 6-8.

◆ GRITT-U-CORNI ALFREDO ◆

1	20-ounce package fettucini
1	cup cooked grits (page 12)
1	cup milk
1	cup ricotta or cottage cheese
1	egg yolk
1/2	teaspoon freshly ground black pepper
2	tablespoons butter or margarine, melted
1/2	cup grated Parmesan cheese, divided
	Dash nutmeg, optional

Cook fettucini according to package directions. Drain and set aside. In food processor or blender, blend grits, milk, cottage cheese, egg and pepper.

In saucepan, melt butter over low heat. Add grits mixture and bring to a simmer, stirring occasionally. Stir in all but 6 teaspoons Parmesan cheese. If mixture seems too thick, thin by stirring in a small amount of milk.

Pour mixture over fettucini and toss. Sprinkle each serving with remaining Parmesan cheese and dash nutmeg, if desired.

Calorie cutter: *Use lowfat milk, cottage cheese and diet margarine.*

Serves 6.

◆ STUFFED SHELLS ◆

1	cup cooked grits (page 12)
1	cup ricotta cheese
1-1/2	cups grated Parmesan cheese, divided
1	egg
2	teaspoons salt
1/2	teaspoon black pepper
1	teaspoon garlic powder
1	12-ounce package jumbo shells, cooked and drained
3-4	cups spaghetti or marinara sauce

Combine grits, ricotta, 1/2 cup Parmesan cheese, egg, salt, pepper and garlic powder in bowl. Stuff shells.

Cover bottom of baking dish with tomato sauce. Arrange stuffed shells in dish and pour sauce over all. Cover and bake 25 minutes at 350°F. Uncover, sprinkle with remaining Parmesan cheese. Bake an additional five minutes.

Variation: Add 1 cup chopped, cooked and drained spinach to filling. Continue as above.

Calorie cutter: *Use skim milk ricotta cheese.*

Serves 6-8.

GRITS-A PIZZA

My husband Jeff Justice, a professional comedian from New York who LOVES pizza, jokes about Southerners eating grits pizza. Little did he know!

♦

2   1/4-ounce packages yeast
1   cup warm water (105-115°F)
1   teaspoon sugar
2   tablespoons vegetable oil
2   teaspoons salt
4-5   cups unbleached white flour
1   cup cooked grits, cooled (page 12)
1-2   tablespoons olive oil
1   cup shredded mozzarella cheese
1-2   cups pizza or spaghetti sauce

Toppings:
       Mushrooms, olives, onions, peppers, pineapple, cilantro, eggplant, okra, you name it

In large mixing bowl, dissolve yeast in water. Stir in sugar. Add oil, salt, 2 cups flour and grits. Beat on low speed with mixer until blended. Increase speed to high and beat

for 1 minute. Scrape sides and beat 1 more minute. Stir in 2 more cups flour and beat 1 more minute.

Knead in extra flour until dough is firm, not sticky. Cover and let rise in warm place until doubled in bulk, 50-60 minutes.

Oil one 16-inch (for thick pizza crust) or two 12-inch pizza pans and sprinkle with cornmeal. Punch batter down and divide in half. Shape with hands into one 16-inch or two 12-inch circles. Place on pizza pan(s). Cover and let rise in warm place for 10-15 minutes.

Add sauce, cheese and toppings. Place on bottom rack of cold oven, then bake at 500°F for 17-20 minutes.

Makes 1 16-inch or 2 12-inch pizzas.

◆ GRITS BURGERS ◆

1	cup cooked grits, slightly cooled (page 12)
1	pound firm tofu, drained and mashed
1	envelope dry onion soup mix
1	teaspoon garlic powder
2	eggs, beaten
2	teaspoons tamari or soy sauce
3	tablespoons toasted sesame seeds
3-4	cups dried herb-style stuffing mix
	Butter or oil for frying

Combine all ingredients except stuffing in large bowl. Mix thoroughly with hands. Mix in stuffing a cup at a time until texture is firm enough to form patties. Let sit for five minutes.

Using about 2/3 cup of the mixture per ball, flatten into patties. Heat small amount of oil or butter in pan or skillet. Fry patties until brown or crispy on both sides.

Serves 6.

◆ QUICK TACO ◆ GRITS CASSEROLE

1	cup grits
4	cups water
1	teaspoon salt
2	tablespoons butter or margarine
3	tablespoons dry taco seasoning mix
1	16-ounce can refried beans
1	8-ounce jar taco sauce, divided
2	cups shredded cheddar cheese, divided
12	large tortilla chips, crushed
1-2	cups sour cream
	Sliced black olives

Bring salted water to boil in medium saucepan. Slowly stir in grits. Cover, reduce heat and cook, stirring occasionally until liquid is absorbed according to grits package directions.

Stir in butter and taco seasoning. In small bowl, combine refried beans and 1/3 cup taco sauce.

Spread half of bean mixture in bottom of 2-quart casserole. Top with half the grits mixture, 1 cup cheese and chips. Repeat layers, excluding chips. Bake at 350°F for 20-30 minutes. Remove from oven and top with sour cream and olives. Sprinkle lightly with taco mix and bake again for 5 minutes.

Calorie cutter: *Use lowfat cheese and light sour cream or nonfat yogurt.*

Vegetarians: Use refried beans made without lard.

Serves 6.

VEGE-GRITIAN CHILI

Grits give this a wonderfully authentic corn flavor while the wheat provides a meat-like texture at low cost — all without any added fat or cholesterol.

1	medium yellow onion, diced
2	cloves garlic, minced
3	tablespoons oil
1/2	cup grits
1	cup bulghur (cracked) wheat
2	cups tomato sauce
2	teaspoons cumin
1/2	teaspoon chili powder
1/4	teaspoon oregano
1	teaspoon garlic powder
1/4	teaspoon cayenne pepper or to taste
2	16-ounce cans pinto or kidney beans

In large skillet, sauté onion and garlic in oil over low heat until onion is translucent. Add dry grits and bulghur. Sauté briefly, stirring to coat grains well.

Stir in water, tomato sauce, spices and beans. Cover and let simmer for 40-50 minutes, stirring occasionally. Serve or transfer to a crock pot for easy party fare.

Shortcut: Use 3 tablespoons packaged chili seasoning instead of dry spices.

Serves 6.

◆ SPICY BLACK BEAN GRITS CHILI ◆

1/4	cup olive oil
1	large onion, chopped
5	medium garlic cloves, pressed
2	tablespoons cumin
1/2	cup grits
1	cup bulghur (cracked) wheat
1	28-ounce can tomatoes, coarsely chopped, juice reserved
3-4	cups water
1	medium red bell pepper
2-3	jalapeno peppers, seeded and minced
1	medium zucchini, diced
4	cups canned black beans, drained and rinsed
1	bunch cilantro leaves, chopped
3	tablespoons fresh lime or lemon juice
	Salt and black pepper to taste

In large skillet, sauté onion, garlic and cumin in oil over low heat until onion is translucent. Add dry grits and bulghur. Sauté briefly, stirring to coat grains well.

Place tomato juice in measuring cup and add water to make 4 cups liquid. Pour over grains and stir to mix. Add tomatoes, bell pepper, jalapenos, zucchini, beans and cilantro. Cover and let simmer for 40-50 minutes, stirring occasionally. If necessary, add small amounts of water to fully cook grains.

Just before serving, stir in lime juice, salt and black pepper.

Serves 6-8.

◆ MEXI-CORN ◆
CHEESE CASSEROLE

3-4	cups water
1	teaspoon salt
1/3	cup grits
2	cups brown or white rice
2	cups sour cream
5	green onions, chopped
	Salt and pepper to taste
1	14-1/2 ounce can corn (1-1/2 cups drained)
1-2	4-ounce cans mild green chilies, drained
1	cup Jack cheese, grated
1/4	cup cheddar cheese, grated
3	tablespoons chopped fresh cilantro

Bring salted water to boil in medium saucepan. Stir in rice and grits. Reduce heat to simmer and cover. Cook rice according to package directions for type of rice used. When grains are done, remove and set aside. Preheat oven to 350°F.

In large bowl, mix rice, grits and sour cream. Stir in green onions, salt and pepper. Grease a 1-1/2-quart casserole. Spread 1/2 rice mixture in bottom of casserole. Top with half the corn, half the chilies and half the Jack cheese. Repeat with remaining corn, chilies and Jack cheese. Top with cheddar cheese. Bake covered for 20 minutes, uncovered for 10 more minutes. Sprinkle with cilantro and serve.

Calorie cutter: *Use light sour cream and lowfat cheese.*

Serves 6-8.

GRITS AROUND THE GLOBE

◆ CHINESE ◆
SWEET 'N' SOUR GRITS

1	cup grits
4	cups water
1	teaspoon salt
1	8-ounce can diced pineapple with juice
3/4-1	cup catsup
1/4	cup rice vinegar
3	tablespoons sugar or honey
2	tablespoons tamari or soy sauce
1/2	cup white onion, chopped
1/2	cup green pepper, chopped
1/2	cup sliced water chestnuts
	Optional vegetables: 1/2 cup bamboo shoots, snow peas, broccoli flowerets, thinly-sliced carrots, etc.

Bring salted water to boil in medium saucepan. Slowly stir in grits. Cover, reduce heat and cook, stirring occasionally until liquid is absorbed according to grits package directions.

Drain pineapple, reserving juice. In separate wok or large skillet, blend pineapple juice, catsup, vinegar, sugar or honey and tamari or soy sauce. Bring to a boil over high heat. When it begins boiling, add the onion, peppers, water chestnuts and any other vegetables. Again return to a boil. Add pineapple chunks and stir mixture into grits.

Shortcut: Cook pineapple chunks, water chestnuts and optional vegetables in 1 cup liquid sweet 'n' sour sauce. Stir into grits and serve.

Serves 6.

◆ EGG FRIED GRITS ◆

3	tablespoons vegetable or peanut oil
1	cup chopped green onion
2	eggs, beaten
3	cups cooked grits, cold (page 12)
2	tablespoons tamari or dark soy sauce
1/2	teaspoon ground white pepper (optional)

Preheat wok or large frying pan. Heat the oil. When hot, add onion and eggs. Stir quickly. Immediately add the grits*, pressing it to the sides and bottom to separate.

Stir in tamari or soy sauce and pepper, if desired. Serve topped with stir-fried vegetables.

*If firmer texture is desired, substitute 1 cup cold cooked rice for 1 cup grits.

Serves 6.

DOLMADES
(Stuffed Grape Leaves)

3	tablespoons olive oil
1/2	cup onion, minced
2	cloves garlic, minced
1/2	cup grits
1/2	cup bulghur (cracked) wheat
	Juice of 1 lemon
2	cups water
1	teaspoon salt
2	tablespoons fresh or dried parsley, minced
1	tablespoon tamari or soy sauce
1/2	teaspoon black pepper
15-20	grape leaves

In large skillet, sauté onion and garlic in 1 tablespoon oil over low heat until onion is translucent. Add dry grits and bulghur. Sauté briefly, stirring to coat grains well. Stir in lemon juice, water and salt. Cover and let simmer, stirring occasionally. Cook until grains are slightly chewy.

Remove from heat and stir in remaining olive oil, parsley, tamari and pepper. Preheat oven to 350°F. Wash brine off grape leaves.

To fill, place leaf flat with stem facing you. Place 1-2 tablespoons of filling in center and fold stem over it. Fold the two sides into the center and working from the end closest to you, roll leaf until it is completely wrapped around the filling.

Place seam side down in lightly-oiled 9x13-inch baking pan. Bake for 20 minutes. Serve immediately. Top with lemon tahini sauce (page 38) or plain yogurt.

Calorie cutter: *Use only 1 tablespoon olive oil to sauté. Skip the other 2 tablespoons olive oil.*

Serves 6.

MOUSSAKA

2	*medium eggplants*
1	*cup butter, divided*
1	*large onion, finely chopped*
3	*cloves garlic, pressed*
1	*cup white or brown rice*
1/2	*cup grits*
2	*cups broth from vegetable bouillon*
2-3	*cups tomato sauce*
1/2	*cup chopped parsley or cilantro*
	Pinch cinnamon
	Salt and pepper to taste
4	*tablespoons all-purpose flour*
1-1/2	*cups milk, boiled*
2	*eggs, beaten until frothy*
	Pinch nutmeg
3/4	*cup ricotta or cottage cheese*
3/4	*cup fine bread crumbs*
3/4	*cup grated Parmesan cheese*

Peel eggplants and cut into 1/2-inch slices. Heat small amount of butter in large skillet. Brown eggplant slices, replacing butter as needed. Set aside.

Melt 4 tablespoons butter in saucepan. Sauté onions and garlic until translucent. Stir in rice and grits, coating thoroughly. Add vegetable broth, 2 cups tomato sauce, parsley, cinnamon, salt and pepper. Stir and cover.

Cook, stirring occasionally until grains are soft but slightly chewy. If needed, add more tomato sauce to cook grains fully. Remove from heat. Preheat oven to 375°F.

In separate saucepan, melt 6 tablespoons butter and blend in flour with wire whisk. Slowly add boiling milk, stirring constantly. When thickened and smooth, remove from heat. Let cool slightly, then stir in eggs, nutmeg and ricotta or cottage cheese.

Grease a 3-quart baking dish and sprinkle bottom lightly with bread crumbs. Alternate layers of eggplant and grits mixture, sprinkling each layer with Parmesan cheese and bread crumbs. Pour cheese sauce over top and bake 1 hour or until top is golden. Remove from oven.

Calorie cutter: *Use diet margarine and skim milk ricotta or lowfat cottage cheese.*

Serves 6-8.

◆ INDIAN CURRY CRISPS ◆

1	cup grits
4	cups water
1	teaspoon salt
3	tablespoons butter
1	teaspoon dried minced onion
1	teaspoon garlic powder
1	teaspoon cumin
1/2	teaspoon turmeric
1/4	teaspoon ginger powder
1/2	teaspoon chili powder
1/2	teaspoon coriander
2	teaspoons curry powder
1/4	teaspoon cayenne pepper
2-3	tablespoons tamari or soy sauce
2	tablespoons sesame seeds (optional)
	Salt to taste
	Butter for frying

Bring salted water to boil in medium saucepan. Slowly stir in grits. Cover, reduce heat and cook, stirring occasionally until liquid is absorbed according to grits package directions. Stir in remaining ingredients. Remove from heat.

Let cool until slightly firm. Flatten into thin patties, using about 1/4 cup of mixture. Fry in small amount of butter until crispy on both sides. Serve immediately.

Serve with "Ila's Cilantro Chutney" (page 30).

Serves 6.

Jyoti's Sweet Indian Grits
(Seero)

1/2	cup ghee (clarified butter)
1	cup uncooked grits
1/2	cup milk, warmed slightly
2	cups hot water
1/2	cup sugar
1/2	cup raisins
	Crushed cardamon
	Grated almonds or pistachios

Heat ghee in heavy saucepan over low heat. Stir in grits. Sauté, stirring occasionally until almond colored, about 10-15 minutes. Remove from heat.

Slowly and carefully pour milk into grits. Add two cups hot water, cover and simmer over low heat. When ghee comes up, stir in sugar. Let mixture cook again over slow heat until sugar is dissolved and grits are soft.

Stir in raisins and top with crushed cardamon and/or grated almonds or pistachio.

Serves 6.

◆

My friend Jyoti shared this sweet, nutty-tasting Indian treat traditionally prepared with cream of wheat. Enjoy it with grits — Sai Ram!

◆

AH-SO GOOD VEGETARIAN NORI ROLLS

◆

You can find nori and wasabi at Asian specialty stores and sometimes even in the international section of your grocery store. This is the fun recipe idea that inspired this book.

◆

4	cups water
1	teaspoon salt
1	cup grits
4-5	nori sheets (thin, dried sheets of seaweed)
	Wasabi (Japanese green horseradish paste)
	Water
6	tablespoons rice vinegar or bottled teriyaki marinade
1	teaspoon salt
2	teaspoons sugar
	Thinly-cut vegetable strips for filling (avocado, cucumber, scallions, carrots, red or green peppers, softened shiitake mushrooms)
	Tamari or soy sauce
	Bamboo rolling mat

Bring salted water in medium saucepan. Slowly stir in grits. Cover, reduce heat and cook, stirring occasionally until liquid is absorbed according to grits package directions. Place grits in large bowl and let cool.

Toast nori sheets (if not pretoasted) by passing each sheet lightly over an open flame. Prepare wasabi by mixing 1-2 teaspoons powder with small amount of water to form smooth paste. Cover and let sit for a few minutes.

Heat rice vinegar, salt and sugar briefly to dissolve sugar. Set aside to cool. Pour over cooled grits and toss with wooden spoon.

Place a nori sheet on bamboo rolling mat. Moisten hands and spread 2/3 cup grits evenly over nori, leaving a 1-1/2-inch strip at top edge uncovered. About 2 inches up from bottom, make a horizontal groove across grits and spread with a thin layer of wasabi. Place thin vegetable strips on top of wasabi in 3 lines, each line extending from edge to edge of the nori sheet. (If using carrots, avocados and green onions, make one horizontal line of each vegetable.)

Pick up bottom edge of mat and start rolling toward top using firm, steady pressure to shape the roll. Any grits squeezed out at sides may be corrected later. Do not allow bare strip of nori at top to be covered by grits or roll won't seal properly. If your roll isn't sealing correctly, moisten top edge of nori with a little water. Adjust shape of roll by squeezing gently on mat. Set aside.

Repeat procedure with remaining nori sheets and mixture, varying colored vegetables for interest. With a sharp, wet knife cut each roll into 1-inch slices. Arrange cut side up on platter. Serve with small bowls of tamari or soy sauce and extra wasabi for dipping.

Serves 6-8.

JAPANESE TERIYAKI GRITS

Substitute cooled leftover teriyaki grits for vinegar-based grits in nori rolls (page 82-83).

♦

3-1/2	*cups water*
1/2	*cup bottled teriyaki marinade*
1	*cup grits*
1	*tablespoon sesame oil*
1	*can water chestnuts*
2	*tablespoons chopped green onion*
1/2	*cup chopped red bell pepper*
	Stir-fried or steamed vegetables

Bring water and marinade to boil in medium saucepan. Slowly stir in grits. Cover, reduce heat and cook, stirring occasionally until liquid is absorbed according to grits package directions.

Remove from heat. Add sesame oil, water chestnuts, green onion and red pepper. Cover pan and let sit for a few minutes to heat vegetables and absorb flavors.

Top with stir-fried or steamed veggies.

Serves 6.

ENCHILADA EL-GRITO GRINGO

A recent non-vegetarian dinner guest was delighted with this dish, admitting he expected raw tofu and carrots.

2	tablespoons oil
1	medium yellow onion, diced
3	cloves garlic, minced
1/2	cup grits
1	cup bulghur (cracked) wheat
1	teaspoon salt
3-4	cups water
2	teaspoons cumin
1	teaspoon chili powder
1/4	teaspoon cayenne pepper or to taste
2	cups salsa, divided
10-12	soft flour tortillas
1-1/2	cups Jack or cheddar cheese, grated
1	tablespoon cilantro leaves, chopped

Heat oil in large skillet over medium heat. Sauté onion and garlic in oil until onion is translucent. Add dry grits and bulghur.

Sauté briefly, stirring to coat grains well. Stir in 3 cups water, spices and 1/2 cup salsa. Cover and let simmer, stirring occasionally. Cook until grains are slightly chewy, adding more water if necessary.

Fill tortillas one at a time with 2-3 tablespoons grits mixture and sprinkle with 2 tablespoons cheese. Roll up and place seam side down to a large shallow baking dish. Top with remaining salsa and cheese.

Bake at 350°F for 20 minutes. Garnish with cilantro. Use any leftover grits mixture for a quick chili base or burrito filling.

Calorie cutter: *Sauté onion and garlic in water. Use lowfat cheese.*

Makes 10-12 enchiladas.

◆ EL TACO CORNO ◆

2	tablespoons oil
1	medium yellow onion, diced
3	cloves garlic, minced
1/2	cup grits
1	cup bulghur (cracked) wheat
3-4	cups water
1	teaspoon salt
3	tablespoons taco seasoning mix
1/2	cup salsa
10-12	taco shells

Fillings:

Sour cream, chopped tomatoes, grated cheddar cheese, avocado, cilantro, black olives

Heat oil in large skillet over medium heat. Sauté onion and garlic in oil until onion is translucent. Add dry grits and bulghur. Sauté briefly, stirring to coat grains well. Stir in water, salt, spice mix and salsa. Cover and let simmer, stirring occasionally. Cook until grains are slightly chewy.

Preheat oven to 350°F. Line up taco shells on baking sheet. Place 2-3 tablespoons filling in each and bake for 5-7 minutes. Remove from oven and top with optional fillings above.

Calorie cutter: *Sauté onion and garlic in water. Skip the cheese and sour cream as toppings or use light versions.*

Makes 10-12 tacos.

◆ BURR-GRIT-OS ◆

1	medium yellow onion, diced
3	cloves garlic, minced
2	tablespoons oil
1/2	cup grits
1	cup bulghur (cracked) wheat
3-4	cups water
1	teaspoon salt
2	teaspoons cumin
1	teaspoon chili powder
1	teaspoon garlic powder
1/4	teaspoon cayenne pepper or to taste
1	16-ounce can refried beans, heated through
10-12	flour tortillas

Options:

sour cream, chopped jalapenos, black olives, tomatoes

In large skillet, sauté onion and garlic in oil over low heat until onion is translucent. Add dry grits and bulghur. Sauté briefly, stirring to coat grains well. Stir in water, salt and spices. Cover and let simmer, stirring occasionally.

Cook until grains are slightly chewy. Heat large skillet. Place tortillas one at a time on skillet about 10 seconds on each side. Remove and cover with cloth to keep warm or assemble immediately.

To make burritos, spread 1/4 cup grits mixture, 1/4 cup refried beans and 3 tablespoons of optional ingredients in center of tortilla. Fold bottom of tortilla up slightly, then fold sides to meet in center.

Shortcut: Use 2 tablespoons packaged taco seasoning instead of dry spices.

Vegetarians: Use refried beans with no lard.

Makes 10-12 burritos.

JALAPENO CASSEROLE

Trendy South-west meets Southern grits in this easy casserole.

1	cup grits
4	cups water
1	teaspoon salt
2	cups Jack or pepper cheese, grated
2	eggs, beaten
2	cloves garlic, minced
1	4-ounce jar pimientos
1/4	cup jalapenos, seeded and sliced
	OR
1	4-ounce can green chilies, drained
	Sliced black olives

Bring salted water to boil in medium saucepan. Slowly stir in grits. Cover, reduce heat and cook, stirring occasionally until liquid is absorbed according to grits package directions. Stir in 1-1/2 cups Jack or pepper cheese, eggs, garlic, pimientos and jalapenos or chilies.

Pour into well-greased 2-quart casserole dish. Top with remaining cheese and black olives. Bake uncovered at 350°F for about 35-40 minutes or until lightly browned.

Calorie cutter: *Use lowfat cheese.*

Serves 6.

◆ SPANISH GRITS ◆

2	tablespoons olive oil
1	yellow onion, diced
2	cloves garlic, minced
1	cup chopped green pepper
3	cups cooked grits, cooled (page 12)
2	cups chopped tomatoes OR tomato sauce
1-1/2	teaspoons salt
1	teaspoon paprika
1/2	teaspoon black pepper
	Dash cayenne pepper

Heat oil in large skillet or pot. Sauté onion and garlic in oil over low heat until onion is translucent. Add green pepper and grits. Sauté briefly, stirring to coat grains well. Stir in tomatoes or sauce and spices. Heat through, stirring to separate grits.

Serves 6.

◆ RUSSIAN ◆
MUSHROOM STRO-GRIT-OFF

3	tablespoons butter or margarine
4	cups sliced mushrooms
1	cup cooked grits, warm (page 12)
1	tablespoon onion bouillon powder
2	cups sour cream
1	teaspoon garlic powder
1	tablespoon tamari or soy sauce
	Dash paprika
1	12-ounce package wide egg noodles, cooked and drained

Heat butter in large skillet. Sauté mushrooms. While mushrooms are cooking, place grits, bouillon and 1 cup sour cream in blender or food processor and blend or beat until creamy. Add garlic powder and tamari, blending thoroughly.

Thin with sour cream to desired consistency. When mushrooms are soft, pour sour cream mixture into skillet. Stir to mix. Let mixture heat slightly. Toss with noodles and sprinkle with paprika.

Calorie cutter: *Use light sour cream.*

Serves 6.

TABOULI SALAD

2	cups boiling water
1/2	teaspoon salt
1	cup bulghur (cracked) wheat
1	cup cooked grits, warm (page 12)
1	cup minced parsley
1/2	cup minced scallions
2-3	teaspoons dried mint or basil or 2 tablespoons fresh herbs
1/4	cup olive oil
	Juice of 1-2 lemons
1	ripe tomato, chopped (optional)
	Salt and pepper to taste

Pour boiling salted water over bulghur in medium bowl. Let sit for 15 minutes to absorb water. Stir in warm grits and mix. Toss all other ingredients into the grain mixture. Add salt and pepper to taste.

Chill for 30 minutes or more to enhance flavor. Serve on lettuce as salad or stuff in pita bread for sandwiches.

See page 51 for an exciting variation.

Serves 6.

I first tasted tabouli in the early '80s at The Laughing Man restaurant in Nashville when I sang backup with Tammy Wynette. This is my grits tribute to those many late night take-outs to the Hall Of Fame Hotel.

◆ FALAFEL GRIT-TLE CAKES ◆

1	cup cooked grits (page 12)
2	slices firm whole wheat bread, crusts removed
2	tablespoons fresh lemon juice
2	tablespoons unbleached white flour
2	tablespoons tahini (sesame paste) or olive oil
3	garlic cloves, pressed
1	egg
2	tablespoons parsley, chopped
1	teaspoon salt
1/4	teaspoon black pepper
1/2	teaspoon ground cumin
1/4	teaspoon turmeric
1/4	teaspoon basil
1	15-ounce can garbanzo beans, drained
	Cayenne pepper to taste
	Oil or margarine for frying

In blender or food processor, blend all ingredients except garbanzo beans until smooth. Add garbanzo beans and blend only to a rough consistency — not too smooth.

Add cayenne pepper to taste. Heat 1-2 tablespoons of oil or margarine in skillet or griddle. Pour 1/2 cup mixture on skillet for each pattie. Brown on each side. Serve with plain yogurt or lemon tahini dressing (page 38).

Serves 6-8.

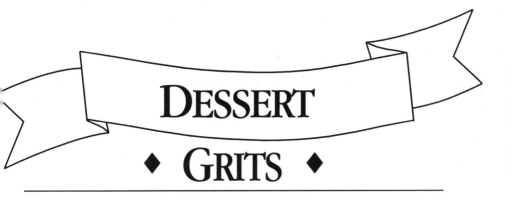

DESSERT
◆ GRITS ◆

EASY OIL PASTRY CRUST

◆

*Two easy
and reliable
pie crusts
used in the
following
delicious
grits pie
recipes.*

◆

1	cup whole wheat flour
1	cup unbleached white flour
1	teaspoon salt
1/2	cup oil
1/4	cup cold water
2	9-inch pie plates

Mix flour and salt in bowl. Combine oil and water and mix into flour with fork. Form into 2 balls with hands. Cover with a cloth and let sit for 5 minutes.

Roll out between sheets of waxed paper. Place rolled dough into pie plates. For prebaked pie shells, prick with fork and bake at 375°F for 10-12 minutes.

Makes 2 9-inch pie crusts.

GRAHAM CRACKER CRUST

1-1/4	cups fine graham cracker crumbs
2	tablespoons sugar
1/3	cup butter or margarine, melted

Combine crumbs and sugar. Add melted butter and mix well. With back of spoon, press firmly on bottom and sides of 9-inch pie pan or springform pan.

Bake in 300°F oven for 5-8 minutes. Allow to cool before filling.

Makes 1 9-inch pie crust.

◆ SECRET PECAN PIE ◆

1/2	cup butter or margarine, melted
1/2	cup sugar
3/4	cup light or dark brown sugar
1	cup light corn syrup
1	cup cooked grits, warm (page 12)
4	eggs, beaten
2	teaspoons vanilla
1/4	teaspoon salt
1	cup chopped pecans
2	9-inch pie crusts, unbaked
2	cups pecan halves

Preheat oven to 325°F. Combine butter, sugars and corn syrup in saucepan. Cook over low heat, stirring constantly until sugar is dissolved. Stir in grits.

Place mixture in large mixing bowl or food processor. Beat or blend until smooth. Add eggs, vanilla and salt and blend again. Stir in chopped pecans.

Pour into pie crusts. Arrange 1 cup pecans on top of each pie. Bake for 55-65 minutes.

Makes 2 pies.

◆ FLORIDA KEY LIME ◆ CREAM PIE

◆

Read Hemingway's 'The Great Grits-by' while baking.

◆

1/2	*cup cooked grits (page 12)*
3/4	*cup lime juice (key lime when in season)*
1	*14-ounce can sweetened condensed milk*
4	*eggs, separated*
1	*9-inch graham cracker pie crust*
6	*tablespoons sugar*

Preheat oven to 350°F. In food processor or blender, blend grits, lime juice and condensed milk until smooth. Add 4 egg yolks and blend again. Beat one egg white until stiff and fold into mixture. Pour into unbaked pie shell.

To make meringue, beat remaining egg whites until stiff, gradually adding sugar. Spread over pie filling, sealing edges. Bake for 20-25 minutes until top is golden. Cool on wire rack and chill before serving, if desired.

Makes 1 pie.

◆ CARROT CAKE ◆

1-1/2	cups unbleached white flour
2/3	cup whole wheat flour
1-1/2	teaspoons baking soda
2	teaspoons baking powder
1/2	teaspoon nutmeg
2	teaspoons cinnamon
1/2	teaspoon ground ginger
1	teaspoon salt
1	cup honey
1/2	cup brown sugar, packed
1	cup buttermilk
1	cup cooked grits (page 12)
4	eggs
3/4	cup oil
1	teaspoon vanilla
2	cups carrots, grated
1/2	cup raisins
1	cup chopped nuts
1	8-ounce can crushed pineapple, drained

Preheat oven to 350°F. Combine flours, baking soda, baking powder, nutmeg, cinnamon, ginger and salt in large bowl. In food processor or mixing bowl, blend or beat honey, brown sugar, buttermilk, grits, eggs, oil and vanilla until creamy. Stir in remaining ingredients. Mix wet and dry ingredients thoroughly.

Pour batter into 3 greased and floured 9-inch layer pans or one 9x13-inch pan. Bake for 35-40 minutes. Test doneness with toothpick or fork inserted in center. Cool in pan for 10 minutes, then cool thoroughly on wire rack. Spread with cream cheese icing (see page 100).

Makes one 3-layered cake or 9x13-inch sheet cake.

◆ CREAM CHEESE ICING ◆

1/2	cup butter, softened
1	8-ounce package cream cheese, softened
1	16-ounce package powdered sugar
1	teaspoon vanilla
2	teaspoons orange or lemon peel, grated (optional)

In large mixing bowl, beat butter and cream cheese until fluffy. Add powdered sugar, vanilla and optional ingredients. Mix well.

Variations: Substitute 3-4 tablespoons honey for powdered sugar.

Will frost one 3-layered cake or 9x13-inch cake.

◆ PINEAPPLE ◆
UPSIDE-DOWN CAKE

2	20-ounce cans juice-packed crushed pineapple
1	cup honey
1	cup whole wheat flour
1	cup all-purpose flour
1	tablespoon baking powder
1	teaspoon cinnamon
1/4	teaspoon nutmeg
1/2	teaspoon salt
1	cup cooked grits (page 12)
1/2	cup vanilla yogurt
1/3	cup butter or margarine, melted
2	eggs
2	teaspoons vanilla

Drain pineapple in a strainer. You should get about 2-1/3 cups juice. Save for use below. Mix drained pineapple and 1/2 cup honey. Grease an 8x8-inch baking pan (preferably glass). Pour in the pineapple mixture.

Preheat the oven to 350°F. Mix dry ingredients in a large bowl. In another large bowl mix 1/2 cup pineapple juice with remaining 1/2 cup honey and all other ingredients. Stir thoroughly.

Combine wet and dry ingredients and mix well. Pour over the pineapple in baking pan. Bake for 40-45 minutes or until a toothpick or fork inserted in center comes out clean. Watch to avoid burning.

Cool for 15-20 minutes, then turn over onto a plate for serving.

Serves 24-36.

Every Christmas Aunt Jane bakes this scrumptious apple torte (sans grits) at her home in Charleston, West Virginia and brings it to St. Louis. It's a good thing Uncle Bob's not like my husband — that cake would be gone before the first state line!

AUNT JANE'S BAVARIAN APPLE TORTE

Pastry:

1/2	cup butter or margarine
1/3	cup sugar
1/4	teaspoon vanilla
1	cup cooked grits, cooled (page 12)

Filling:

1	8-ounce package cream cheese, softened
1/4	cup sugar
1	egg
1/2	teaspoon vanilla

Fruit layer:

1/3	cup sugar
1/2	teaspoon cinnamon
4	cups peeled, thinly-sliced Golden Delicious apples

Topping:

1/2	cup sour cream
1	tablespoon sugar
	Dash cinnamon

In mixing bowl, cream butter, sugar, vanilla and grits. Blend in flour. Spread dough onto bottom and sides of 9-inch springform pan.

In separate bowl, combine cream cheese and sugar, mixing well. Blend in egg and vanilla. Pour into pastry-lined pan. Combine sugar and cinnamon. Toss apples in sugar mixture. Spoon over cream cheese layer.

Bake at 450°F for 10 minutes. Reduce heat to 400°F and bake 25-30 more minutes. While cake is baking, prepare topping by mixing 1/2 cup sour cream with sugar. Remove torte from oven. Spread topping over apples and sprinkle lightly with cinnamon. Bake 5 more minutes.

Cool before removing rim from pan.

Serves 6-8.

◆ APPLESAUCE CAKE ◆

1-2/3   *cups whole wheat pastry flour*
2   *teaspoons baking powder*
1/2   *teaspoon salt*
1   *teaspoon cinnamon*
1/4   *teaspoon cloves*
1/4   *teaspoon allspice*
3   *eggs*
2/3   *cup safflower oil*
1/2   *cup honey*
1   *cup cooked grits (page 12)*
1   *cup applesauce*
1/2   *cup raisins*
1/2   *cup chopped walnuts*

Icing:

1   *8-ounce package cream cheese, softened*
1   *16-ounce package powdered sugar*
1/2   *cup butter or margarine*
1/4   *teaspoon cinnamon*
1/8   *teaspoon nutmeg*
1/8   *teaspoon allspice*

Preheat oven to 350°F. In large mixing bowl, mix flour, baking powder, salt and spices. Beat egg yolks in separate bowl. Add oil, honey and grits. Mix thoroughly. Add applesauce, raisins, and nuts and mix again.

Add wet mixture to dry ingredients and mix well. Beat egg whites until stiff but not dry. Fold into the batter (do not overmix). Grease the bottom of an 8x8-inch baking pan. Pour in the batter.

Bake for 35-40 minutes until a toothpick or fork comes out clean when inserted. Let cool. Prepare icing by beating all ingredients in mixer or food processor until smooth. Spread cake evenly with icing and serve.

Serves 24-36.

GOOEY BUTTER CHESS CAKE

1	box yellow butter cake mix
2	eggs
1/2	cup butter or margarine, melted
1	cup cooked grits (page 12)
1	8-ounce package cream cheese
1	16-ounce package powdered sugar
2	eggs
1	teaspoon vanilla

Preheat oven to 350°F. Combine first 4 ingredients in large mixing bowl. Beat thoroughly.

Spread mixture in well-greased 9x13-inch baking pan. Beat next 4 ingredients until smooth and creamy. Pour over cake batter.

Bake for 35-45 minutes. Cool and cut into bars. Topping will be "gooey."

Serves 24-36.

◆

My mom used to go to a bakery for this favorite St. Louis cake. Now she can go to the kitchen!

◆

◆ CINNAMON CRUMB ◆ COFFEE CAKE

Topping:

1/3	cup brown sugar
1/2	cup sugar
1	tablespoon flour
3	tablespoons butter or margarine, softened
1	teaspoon cinnamon

Batter:

1/2	cup butter or margarine, softened
1	cup cooked grits, cooled (page 12)
3/4	cup sugar
2	eggs
1/2	teaspoon vanilla
2	cups all-purpose flour
1/2	teaspoon salt
1	teaspoon baking powder
1	teaspoon baking soda
1	cup sour cream

Mix topping ingredients thoroughly and set aside. Grease a 9-inch round or square baking pan. Preheat oven to 350°F. In mixing bowl, beat butter, grits and sugar until fluffy. Add eggs and vanilla and beat well.

In separate bowl, mix flour, salt, baking powder and soda. Add dry mixture to wet in parts, alternating with sour cream and mixing thoroughly. Pour batter into prepared pan. Sprinkle with topping. Bake 40-45 minutes until toothpick inserted in center comes out clean.

Variation: Fold 1 cup fresh blueberries into batter before pouring into pan.

Serves 6.

◆ SPICE CAKE ◆

2	cups whole wheat pastry flour
1-1/2	cups brown sugar, packed
1	teaspoon baking powder
1-1/4	teaspoons baking soda
1/2	teaspoon salt
2	teaspoons cinnamon
3/4	teaspoon cloves
1/2	teaspoon nutmeg
1/2	cup butter or margarine, softened
1/4	cup oil
2	eggs
1	cup cooked grits (page 12)
1	cup sour cream
1	cup raisins
1/2	cup chopped walnuts

Icing:

1	8-ounce package cream cheese, softened
1	stick butter or margarine
1	tablespoon lemon juice
1	16-ounce box powdered sugar

Preheat oven to 350°F. In large mixing bowl, mix flour, baking powder and soda, salt and spices. In separate bowl or food processor, beat or blend butter, oil, eggs, grits and sour cream until creamy. Add raisins and nuts. Stir to mix.

Add wet mixture to dry ingredients and blend well. Grease and flour a 9x13-inch baking pan. Pour in the batter. Bake for 40-45 minutes until a toothpick or fork comes out clean when inserted. Let cool.

To make icing, beat softened cream cheese, butter and lemon juice. Slowly add powdered sugar until smooth. Spread cake evenly with icing and serve.

Serves 24-36.

NEW YORK CHERRY CHEESECAKE

Send some to your Yankee friends and let them try it. THEN tell them ...

◆

Filling:

1	cup cooked grits, cooled (page 12)
2	8-ounce packages cream cheese, softened
3	eggs
2/3	cup sugar
1	tablespoon fresh lemon juice
1	teaspoon vanilla extract

Crust:

1	recipe Graham Cracker Crust in 9-inch springform pan (page 96)

Topping:

1/2	cup sour cream
1	21-ounce can cherry pie filling

Preheat oven to 450°F. Place filling ingredients in large mixing bowl or food processor and beat or blend 8-10 minutes until smooth. Pour mixture into prebaked pie crust.

Bake for 10 minutes at 450°F, reduce heat to 350°F and bake 45-55 minutes until center is set. Remove from oven and top with sour cream. Return to oven for 5 more minutes. Cool on wire rack for an hour, then refrigerate overnight. Top with pie filling before serving. Refrigerate leftovers.

Variation: Top with other fruit pie fillings before serving.

Serves 12-16.

PUFFY CHERRY TREAT

1	cup cooked grits (page 12)
1	cup milk
2	eggs
1/2	cup biscuit baking mix
1/4	cup sugar
1/2	teaspoon vanilla
2	tablespoons butter or margarine, softened
1	21-ounce can cherry pie filling

◆

A wonderful lowfat treat I adapted from a recipe on a cherry pie filling can.

◆

Preheat oven to 400°F. In food processor or mixing bowl, blend or beat all ingredients except pie filling for 1 minute.

Pour ingredients into greased 10-inch pie pan or 11x7-inch baking pan. Spoon pie filling over top. Bake 30-35 minutes until golden brown.

Calorie cutter: *Use lowfat milk, diet margarine and light pie filling.*

Serves 6-8.

◆ DOUBLE FUDGY BROWNIES ◆

1	cup cooked grits (page 12)
1	cup butter or margarine, melted
1/4	cup oil
2	cups sugar
1	cup unbleached white flour
3/4	cup baking cocoa powder (unsweetened)
1/2	teaspoon baking soda
1/2	teaspoon salt
4	eggs
3	teaspoons vanilla, divided
1	cup chopped nuts
1	12-ounce package semi-sweet chocolate chips
1	14-ounce can sweetened condensed milk

Preheat oven to 350°F. Grease a 13x9-inch baking pan. In food processor or mixing bowl blend or beat grits, butter and oil until creamy. In separate bowl mix together sugar, flour, cocoa powder, soda and salt. Combine wet and dry mixtures, stirring until smooth.

Stir in eggs and 2 teaspoons vanilla just until smooth. Fold in nuts. Pour batter into pan. Bake for 18-20 minutes until brownies start to pull away from edges of pan.

Just before brownies are done, melt chocolate chips with sweetened condensed milk and remaining vanilla in heavy saucepan. Immediately spread over hot brownies. Cool thoroughly and cut into bars.

Makes 36-40 brownies.

◆ CHOCOLATE ◆ PECAN BARS

1	box yellow cake mix
2	eggs
1/2	cup butter or margarine, melted
1	cup cooked grits (page 12)
1	cup chopped pecans
1	6-ounce package chocolate chips
1	8-ounce package cream cheese
1	16-ounce package powdered sugar
2	eggs
1	teaspoon vanilla

Preheat oven to 350°F. Combine first 4 ingredients in large mixing bowl. Beat well. Spread mixture in well-greased 9x13-inch baking pan. Sprinkle with chocolate chips and chopped pecans.

Beat remaining ingredients until smooth and creamy. Pour over cake batter. Bake for 40-50 minutes. Bars should be slightly sticky. Cool and cut into bars.

Serves 16-24.

◆ ROCKY ROAD BARS ◆

Filling:

1	cup semi-sweet chocolate chips
1	14-ounce can sweetened condensed milk
1	cup cooked grits, hot (page 12)
1	cup chopped nuts

Crust and topping:

1	cup butter or margarine, softened
1-1/3	cups brown sugar, firmly packed
1-1/2	teaspoons vanilla
2-1/2	cups rolled oats
1	cup all-purpose flour
1/2	teaspoon baking soda
1/4	teaspoon salt
1-1/2	cups walnuts, chopped
1	3-ounce jar marshmallow creme

Preheat oven to 375°F. Butter a 9x13-inch pan. In medium saucepan, melt chocolate chips with sweetened condensed milk. Remove from heat. Stir in hot grits and nuts.

In mixing bowl, beat butter, sugar and vanilla until fluffy. Add remaining ingredients, except marshmallow creme. Blend until evenly mixed and crumbly. Reserve 2 cups.

Press remaining crumb mixture onto bottom of pan. Spread a layer of marshmallow creme over crust. Next pour a layer of chocolate mixture and sprinkle with remaining crumbs.

Bake 25-35 minutes. Cool thoroughly. Cut into bars.

Serves 24-36.

◆ SEVEN (*And a Half*) ◆ LAYER BARS

1/2	cup butter or margarine
1-1/2	cups graham cracker crumbs
1	cup semi-sweet chocolate chips
1	cup shredded coconut
1	cup butterscotch chips
1	cup pecans, chopped
1/2	cup cooked grits (page 12)
1	14-ounce can sweetened condensed milk

Preheat oven to 350°F. Melt butter in 9x13-inch baking pan. Sprinkle crumbs evenly over melted margarine. Layer chocolate chips, coconut, butterscotch chips and pecans.

In blender or food processor, blend grits and condensed milk. Pour mixture evenly over top of layers. Bake for 30-35 minutes. While still warm, cut into 1-1/2-inch squares. Cool in pan on wire rack.

Serves 24-36.

◆ PEANUT BUTTER ◆ CHOCOLATE BARS

Filling:
1	cup cooked grits, hot (page 12)
1/2	cup peanut butter
1	14-ounce can sweetened condensed milk
1	tablespoon lemon juice

Crust and topping:
2-1/2	cups rolled oats
1-1/2	cups all-purpose flour
1	cup dry roasted peanuts, chopped
1	cup brown sugar, firmly packed
1	teaspoon baking soda
1/4	teaspoon salt
1	cup butter or margarine, softened
1	cup semi-sweet chocolate chips

Preheat oven to 375°F. Combine first 4 ingredients in large bowl. Mix thoroughly and set aside. Mix rolled oats, flour, peanuts, sugar, soda and salt. Add softened margarine and mix until it resembles coarse crumbs. Reserve 2 cups.

Press remaining mixture onto bottom of 9x13-inch greased pan. Bake for 12 minutes. Remove from oven and spread filling mixture to within 1/2 inch of edges.

Mix remaining crumbs with chocolate chips. Sprinkle over top. Press lightly. Bake for 20-25 minutes until golden brown. Cool in pan on wire rack. Cut into bars and serve.

Serves 24-36.

OAT-RAISIN BARS

Filling:

1	cup cooked grits (page 12)
2	cups raisins
1	14-ounce can sweetened condensed milk
1	tablespoon lemon juice

Crust and topping:

1	cup butter or margarine, softened
1-1/3	cups brown sugar, firmly packed
1-1/2	teaspoons vanilla
2-1/2	cups rolled oats
1	cup all-purpose flour
1-1/2	cups walnuts, chopped
1/2	teaspoon baking soda
1/4	teaspoon salt

Preheat oven to 375°F. In medium saucepan, combine first 4 ingredients. Cook over medium heat until bubbles form. Remove from heat and set aside to cool slightly. Beat butter, sugar and vanilla until fluffy. Add remaining ingredients and blend until evenly mixed and crumbly. Reserve 2 cups.

Press remaining crumb mixture onto bottom of 9x13-inch greased pan. Spread raisin mixture to within 1/2 inch of edges. Sprinkle with remaining oat mixture. Pat lightly. Bake 25-35 minutes or until golden brown.

Cool thoroughly. Cut into bars.

Serves 24-36.

♦

A chewy bar cookie that's perfect for lunch boxes or snacks. My editor Gail's version of health food — it's got raisins, right?

♦

SOUTHERN PECAN PIE BARS

◆

Pecan pie taste without the fuss of a pastry crust.

◆

Crust:

1-1/2	cups all-purpose flour
1/2	cup rolled oats
1/3	cup brown sugar
3/4	cup butter or margarine, softened

Filling:

4	eggs, beaten
1	cup pecans, coarsely chopped
1/2	cup brown sugar
1/4	teaspoon salt
1	cup light corn syrup
1	teaspoon vanilla
1	cup cooked grits, warm (page 12)
2	tablespoons all-purpose flour

Preheat oven to 350°F. Mix flour, oats, and brown sugar. Cut in butter until mixture resembles coarse crumbs. Press mixture into greased 9x13-inch pan. Bake for 15 minutes.

In medium bowl, beat eggs slightly. Add remaining ingredients and mix thoroughly. Pour mixture into crust. Bake 30-35 minutes. Cool in pan on wire rack.

Serves 24-36.

◆ CUSTARD'S LAST STAND ◆

1	*cup cooked grits (page 12)*
1	*cup cottage cheese*
1	*cup vanilla yogurt*
2	*eggs*
1/2	*cup honey*
1	*teaspoon vanilla*
1/2	*teaspoon salt*
1/2	*cup raisins*

Topping:

1/4	*cup light brown sugar*
1/3	*cup all-purpose flour*
2	*tablespoons butter, softened*

Preheat oven to 350°F. Blend cooked grits and cottage cheese in food processor or blender until smooth. Add yogurt, eggs, honey, vanilla and salt. Blend again until creamy.

Place raisins in bottom of 1-1/2-quart greased casserole. Pour custard mixture over raisins. Bake uncovered for 25 minutes. Mix topping ingredients until mixture resembles coarse meal. Sprinkle on top and return to oven. Bake 15 minutes longer.

Serves 6.

TAPIOCA
GRITS PUDDING

◆

An economical version of this traditional dessert.

◆

2	cups milk
4	tablespoons grits
1/2	teaspoon salt
1/4	cup sugar
5	tablespoons all-purpose flour
2	eggs, beaten
1/2	teaspoon vanilla

Place milk in heavy saucepan. Stir in grits and salt. Cook and stir over medium heat and let simmer about 10 minutes. Meanwhile combine sugar and flour in bowl. Add beaten eggs and 3 tablespoons hot milk, mixing thoroughly. Place sugar mixture into pan with milk and grits, stirring constantly until very thick.*

Pour mixture into dessert dishes or large casserole. Cover surface of pudding with plastic wrap. Refrigerate until chilled. Pudding thickens as it cools. If creamier texture is desired, stir before serving. Sprinkle with nutmeg or cinnamon if you like.

*Note: Mixture will have consistency and taste of tapioca. If smoother pudding is desired, place warm mixture in blender or food processor and blend 8-10 minutes until smooth. Continue as above.

Serves 4-6.

◆ HAWAIIAN ◆
TROPI-GRITS PUDDING

1	13-ounce can coconut milk
2	cups milk
1	8-ounce can crushed pineapple, drained with juice reserved
1/2	teaspoon salt
1	cup grits
2	eggs, beaten
1/2	cup sugar
1	teaspoon vanilla
1-1/2	cups flaked coconut
	Finely-chopped macadamia nuts (optional)

Place coconut milk, milk, pineapple juice and salt in large saucepan over low heat. Bring to simmer and stir in grits*, eggs, sugar and vanilla. Continue to simmer, stirring occasionally until mixture thickens (about 10 minutes). Stir in coconut and pineapple. Serve warm and top each serving with optional grated nuts.

*If cold pudding is desired, reduce amount of grits to 1/2 cup. Continue as above and refrigerate 4 hours or overnight. Blend briefly before serving, thinning with small amount of milk if needed.

Variation: If (like my mom) you're not a coconut lover, use only the pineapple juice, adding regular milk to make 4 cups liquid. Continue as above and skip the flaked coconut.

Serves 6.

◆ BANANA CREAM ◆ COOKIE PUDDING

4	cups milk, divided in half
1/2	cup grits
2	3-ounce packages vanilla pudding mix (not instant)
2	eggs, beaten
1-1/2	12-ounce boxes vanilla wafers
6	ripe bananas, thinly sliced

Place 2 cups milk and grits in medium saucepan over low heat. Bring to simmer and stir cook grits about 10 minutes. Slowly stir in remaining milk and pudding mix. Continue to simmer, stirring occasionally until mixture thickens. Remove from heat. Let cool. Place in blender or food processor and blend until creamy.

Layer bottom of 9x13-inch pan with vanilla wafers. Cover wafers with layer of bananas, then layer of custard. Alternate layers, ending with custard on top. Refrigerate for 4 hours or overnight.

Serves 12-16.

GRITS KUGEL
(Sweet Noodle Pudding)

1	8-ounce package wide egg noodles
1	cup cooked grits, warm (page 12)
3	eggs, beaten
1/2	cup sugar
1	teaspoon vanilla
1	teaspoon cinnamon
1/4	cup melted butter
1/4	teaspoon salt
1	cup sour cream
1/2	cup milk
2	cups creamed cottage cheese
1	8-ounce can crushed pineapple
1/2	cup raisins

My friend Fran serves this traditional Jewish dish which I've adapted to grits.

Cook noodles according to package directions. Drain and set aside.

In large mixing bowl, beat remaining ingredients except pineapple and raisins. Stir noodles, pineapple and raisins into mixture.

Pour into a well-buttered 2-quart baking dish. Bake at 350°F for an hour or until top is golden.

Calorie cutter: *Use light sour cream or nonfat vanilla yogurt, lowfat cottage cheese and diet margarine.*

Serves 6-8.

◆ VAN GRITS ◆
DUTCH APPLESAUCE

2-1/2	*cups water*
1	*teaspoon salt*
1-1/2	*cups frozen apple juice concentrate, thawed*
1	*cup grits*
3	*tablespoons butter or margarine*
1/4	*cup brown sugar*
1/2	*teaspoon cinnamon*
1/4	*teaspoon allspice*

Options:
1/2	*cup each grated apple and/or raisins*

Bring salted water and apple juice to boil in medium saucepan. Slowly stir in grits. Cover, reduce heat and cook, stirring occasionally until liquid is absorbed according to grits package directions. Stir in brown sugar, cinnamon and allspice. Swirl in apples and raisins, if desired.

Serves 6.

◆ CRISPY ◆
CINNAMON APPLE SQUARES

1	*recipe "Van Grits Dutch Applesauce" (above)*
	Butter for frying
	Powdered sugar

Pour prepared recipe into 9x13-inch pan. Cover with plastic wrap. Let cool in refrigerator at least 4 hours or overnight. Cut into 2-inch squares.

Heat small amount of butter in large skillet. Fry apple squares until crispy on both sides. Sprinkle lightly with powdered sugar and serve.

Serves 6.

◆ GEORGIA PEACH COBBLER ◆

1/2   cup butter, melted
1   cup all-purpose flour
1   teaspoon baking powder
1   teaspoon baking soda
1   cup sugar
1/2   teaspoon salt
1   cup milk
1/2   cup cooked grits, warm (page 12)
1   21-ounce can peach pie filling

Preheat oven to 350°F. Pour butter in 9x13-inch baking pan, tilting to cover bottom. In mixing bowl, thoroughly combine flour, baking powder, baking soda, sugar and salt. Stir in milk and grits.

Pour batter evenly over melted butter. Add pie filling evenly on top of batter. Do not stir. Bake for 35-45 minutes until browned. Cool slightly before serving.

Serves 6.

HOLIDAY

◆ GRITTINGS ◆

◆ NEW YEAR'S EVE ◆ EGGNOG PUDDING

4	*cups prepared eggnog**
1/2	*cup grits*
	Sugar
1/2	*teaspoon rum extract*
	Dash nutmeg or cinnamon

Bring eggnog to simmer in medium saucepan. Stir in grits. Cover and cook, stirring occasionally until grits soften, 8-10 minutes. Remove from heat. Stir in sugar, if needed and rum extract. Let cool slightly and place mixture in blender or food processor. Blend until creamy.

Pour mixture into dessert dishes or large casserole. Cover surface of pudding with plastic wrap. Refrigerate until chilled. Pudding thickens as it cools. If creamier texture is desired, stir before serving. Sprinkle with nutmeg or cinnamon.

*Note: You can make this recipe out of season using canned eggnog.

Serves 6.

◆ VALENTINE HEART ◆ WITH RASPBERRY PURÉE

3	cups milk
1/2	teaspoon salt
3/4	cup grits
2	eggs, beaten
1/2	cup sugar
1	teaspoon vanilla
1	teaspoon almond extract
6	drops red food coloring (optional)
1	10 or 12-ounce package frozen raspberries, thawed
2	tablespoons sugar
1	teaspoon cornstarch

Place milk and salt in large saucepan over low heat. Bring to simmer and stir in grits, eggs and sugar. Continue to simmer, stirring occasionally until mixture thickens and grits are soft (10-15 minutes).

Remove from heat. Stir in vanilla, almond extract and red food coloring, if desired. Pour grits into greased 3-cup heart-shaped mold. Let cool in refrigerator 4-6 hours or overnight.

To make purée, drain raspberries, reserving juice. In food processor or blender, lightly puree raspberries. Remove to bowl. Stir in sugar, 3 tablespoons juice and cornstarch. Chill in refrigerator for 2 or more hours.

When mold is ready, invert onto platter and top with chilled raspberry purée.

Makes 1 heart.

◆ GEORGE WASHING-GRIT ◆ CHERRY CRISP

3/4   *cup all-purpose flour*
3/4   *cup brown sugar*
6   *tablespoons butter or margarine, softened*
1   *21-ounce can cherry pie filling*
2   *cups cooked grits, warm (page 12)*

Preheat oven to 375°F. Mix together flour, sugar and butter until mixture resembles coarse meal. Set aside.

In 2-quart casserole, stir together pie filling and warm grits. Spread crumb mixture on top. Bake 30-40 minutes, uncovered. Serve with vanilla frozen yogurt.

Serves 6.

◆ ST. PADDY'S ◆
IRISH SODA BREAD

3/4	*cup raisins*
1	*cup boiling water*
2-3	*cups unbleached white flour*
1-1/2	*teaspoons baking powder*
1/2	*teaspoon salt*
1/4	*teaspoon baking soda*
1	*cup buttermilk or plain yogurt*
1	*cup cooked grits (page 12)*
3	*tablespoons honey*
1	*tablespoon caraway seeds*

Preheat oven to 350°F. Cover raisins with boiling water and let set 10 minutes. Mix together 2 cups flour, baking powder, salt and baking soda.

In food processor or blender, blend buttermilk, grits and honey. Stir in raisins and caraway seeds. Add wet mixture to flour mixture a little at a time, to make soft and just slightly sticky dough. If too sticky, add small amount of flour.

Knead dough for 1 minute. Form into round ball and place on greased cookie sheet. Cut cross on top with knife.

Bake for 40-50 minutes.

Makes one loaf.

GOBBLIN' PUMPKIN GRITS

1   cup canned pumpkin
1   cup cooked grits, warm (page 12)
2   tablespoons butter or margarine
4   tablespoons brown sugar
1/2   teaspoon cinnamon
1   7-ounce jar marshmallow creme

In food processor or mixing bowl, blend or beat pumpkin and grits until smooth. Pour in saucepan and stir in butter, brown sugar and cinnamon. Heat through.

Place in 1-quart casserole and spread top with marshmallow creme. Broil until top is golden.

Serves 6.

◆

A little decadent, but even my most health-conscious friends scarfed this at dinner one night.

◆

◆ THANKS-GRITTING ◆
STUFFING

1	cup grits
5	cups water, divided
1	teaspoon salt
1/3	cup butter or margarine
1/2	teaspoon thyme
1/4	teaspoon sage
1/2	teaspoon marjoram
1/2	teaspoon onion powder
1/2	teaspoon garlic powder
1	teaspoon chives
1/2	teaspoon celery flakes
1	egg, beaten
1	cup dry herb stuffing mix

Bring 4 cups salted water to boil in medium saucepan. Slowly stir in grits.

Cover, reduce heat and cook, stirring occasionally until liquid is absorbed according to grits package directions. Stir in remaining ingredients and 1 cup water. Let sit for 10 minutes.

Shortcut: Substitute 1 tablespoon poultry seasoning for spices.

Variations: Add 1/2 cup stuffing ingredients — diced celery, raisins, nuts, water chestnuts or other favorite additions.

Serves 6-8.

GRANDMA GINNY'S PUMPKIN PIE

◆

My mother-in-law's best pumpkin pie recipe made even creamier with grits!

◆

2	cups milk, scalded
2	16-ounce cans pumpkin
1	cup cooked grits (page 12)
1-1/4	cups sugar
1/4	teaspoon salt
1	teaspoon ground ginger
1	teaspoon cinnamon
3	eggs
2	9-inch unbaked pie crusts (2-cup volume) (page 96)

Scald milk in medium saucepan. Set aside. Preheat oven to 350°F.

In food processor or blender, blend grits and pumpkin until smooth, about 6 minutes. Add milk and remaining ingredients. Blend again for about 3 minutes until smooth and creamy.

Pour equal amounts of mixture into 2 pie crusts. Bake at for 45-60 minutes until toothpick or fork inserted in center comes out clean.

Vegetarians: If using premade pie crusts, use ones made without lard.

Serves 12-16.

QUICK PUMPKIN CREAM PIE

1	30-ounce can pumpkin pie mix
1	cup cooked grits (page 12)
3	eggs, beaten
2/3	cup undiluted evaporated milk
2	9-inch unbaked pie crusts (2-cup volume) (page 96)

Preheat oven to 350°F. In food processor or blender, blend pumpkin pie mix and grits until smooth, about 6 minutes. Add eggs and milk and blend again until smooth and creamy. Pour equal amounts of mixture into 2 pie crusts.

Bake 50-60 minutes until toothpick or fork inserted in center comes out clean.

Vegetarians: If using premade pie crusts, use ones made without lard.

Serves 12-16.

◆

Don't tell Grandma Ginny you made the quick one!

◆

◆ CREAMY CHRISTMAS ◆ CHEESECAKE COOKIES

Crust and topping:

1/2	cup butter or margarine, softened
1/2	cup brown sugar, firmly packed
1-1/2	cups all-purpose flour
1	cup pecans, chopped fine
1/2	teaspoon baking soda
1/4	teaspoon salt

Filling:

1	cup cooked grits, cooled (page 12)
1	8-ounce package cream cheese
1/3	cup sugar
1	egg
1	tablespoon lemon juice
1/2	teaspoon vanilla
	Red and green candied cherries, halved

Preheat oven to 350°F. Grease an 8x8-inch baking pan. In large mixing bowl, beat butter and sugar until fluffy. Add flour, pecans, baking soda and salt. Blend until evenly mixed and crumbly. Reserve 1 cup. Press remaining mixture in bottom of pan. Bake for 12 minutes.

In food processor or mixing bowl, blend or beat grits, cream cheese and sugar until creamy. Add egg, lemon juice and vanilla and blend again. Pour filling over baked bottom layer. Sprinkle with reserved crumb mixture. Top with candied cherries. Bake another 20 minutes.

Cool in pan on wire rack. Cut into 2x2-inch bars. Refrigerate before serving.

Serves 12-16.

BREADS

APPLE BRAN MUFFINS

2/3	cup raisins
1-1/4	cups frozen apple juice concentrate, thawed
1	cup whole wheat flour
1-1/2	cups unbleached white flour
1/2	cup wheat bran
1/2	cup wheat germ
1	teaspoon cinnamon
1-1/2	teaspoons baking soda
1-1/2	cups buttermilk or plain yogurt
1	cup cooked grits (page 12)
1/2	cup honey
3	eggs
1/4	cup butter or margarine, melted
1/2	cup nuts
1	cup finely-chopped apple

Place raisins and 1/2 cup apple juice in small saucepan and simmer 5 minutes over low heat. Set aside.

Preheat oven to 400°F. In large bowl, combine flours, bran, wheat germ, cinnamon and baking soda. In food processor or mixing bowl, blend or beat buttermilk, grits, remaining apple juice, honey, eggs and margarine.

Combine wet and dry ingredients. Fold in apple and nuts.

Fill greased muffin tins 2/3 full with batter. Bake for 25-30 minutes until golden brown.

Makes about 24 muffins.

◆ NUTTY BANANA MUFFINS ◆

1	cup whole wheat flour
2	cups unbleached white flour
1-1/2	teaspoons baking soda
1-1/2	cups mashed banana
1	cup buttermilk or plain yogurt
1	cup cooked grits (page 12)
3/4	cup brown sugar
3	eggs
1/4	cup margarine, melted
1	cup chopped walnuts or pecans
1	cup raisins (optional)

Preheat oven to 400°F. In large mixing bowl, combine flours and baking soda. In food processor or mixing bowl, blend or beat remaining ingredients except nuts and optional raisins.

Combine wet and dry ingredients. Fold in nuts and raisins, if desired.

Fill greased muffin tins 2/3 full with batter. Bake for 25-30 minutes until golden brown.

Makes about 24 muffins.

◆ PINEAPPLE ZUCCHINI ◆ GRITS BREAD

2	cups unbleached white flour
1	cup whole wheat flour
1	teaspoon baking soda
1/2	teaspoon baking powder
1	teaspoon nutmeg
2	teaspoons cinnamon
1	teaspoon salt
2	cups brown sugar, packed
2	cups finely shredded zucchini
1	cup cooked grits (page 12)
3	eggs
3/4	cup oil
1	teaspoon vanilla
1	cup walnuts, chopped
1	20-ounce can crushed pineapple, drained

Preheat oven to 350°F.

Combine flours, baking soda, baking powder, nutmeg, cinnamon and salt in large bowl. In large mixing bowl, beat remaining ingredients except nuts and pineapple until creamy. Mix wet and dry ingredients thoroughly. Fold in nuts and pineapple.

Pour batter into 2 greased 9x5-inch loaf pans or 3 8x4-inch pans.

Bake for 60-70 minutes for large loaves, 45-50 minutes for smaller ones. Bread is done when toothpick or fork inserted in center comes out clean. Cool in pan for 10 minutes, then cool thoroughly on wire rack.

Makes 2 large or 3 small loaves.

◆ Pumpkin Nut Raisin Bread ◆

2-1/2	cups unbleached white flour
1	cup whole wheat flour
3	cups sugar
2	teaspoons baking soda
1	teaspoon nutmeg
2	teaspoons cinnamon
1	teaspoon salt
1	16-ounce can pumpkin
1	cup cooked grits (page 12)
4	eggs
1	cup oil
1/3	cup water
1	teaspoon vanilla
1	cup chopped pecans or walnuts
1	cup raisins

Preheat oven to 350°F.

Combine dry ingredients in large bowl. In food processor or mixing bowl, blend or beat remaining wet ingredients until creamy. Stir in nuts and raisins.

Mix wet and dry ingredients thoroughly. Pour into 2 greased 9x5-inch loaf pans.

Bake for 60-70 minutes. Bread is done when toothpick or fork inserted in center comes out clean. Cool in pan for 10 minutes, then cool thoroughly on wire rack.

Makes 2 loaves.

◆ HAWAIIAN ◆
BANANA NUT BREAD

1	cup cooked grits (page 12)
6	ripe bananas, peeled
1/2	cup melted butter or margarine
2	eggs
1-1/2	cups sugar or 1 cup honey
1	teaspoon baking soda
1	teaspoon salt
3	cups whole wheat flour
1	cup unbleached white flour
1	cup nuts

Preheat oven to 325°F. Grease 2 9x5-inch loaf pans.

Blend first 4 ingredients in food processor or blender until well processed, about 6 minutes. Slowly add sugar or honey and blend again.

In large mixing bowl, combine baking soda, salt and flours. Add banana mixture to dry ingredients and mix. Stir in nuts.

Pour even amounts in loaf pans. Bake for 40-50 minutes until toothpick or fork inserted in center of loaf comes out clean.

Makes 2 loaves.

◆ GRITS CORNBREAD ◆

1-1/2	cups yellow cornmeal
1/2	cup unbleached white flour
1/2	teaspoon salt
2	teaspoons baking powder
1	cup cooked grits (page 12)
3	tablespoons melted butter or oil
2	tablespoons honey
1-2	eggs
1-1/2	cups buttermilk or plain yogurt

Preheat oven to 400°F.

Combine dry ingredients in medium bowl. In blender or food processor, blend grits and remaining liquid ingredients until creamy. Combine wet and dry mixtures. Do not overmix.

Pour into a greased 8-inch baking pan. Bake for 35-40 minutes. Cool on a wire rack.

Serves 8-12.

CHEDDAR CORNBREAD

1-1/2	cups yellow cornmeal
1/2	cup unbleached white flour
1/2	teaspoon salt
	Cumin, chili powder and/or cayenne to taste (optional)
2	teaspoons baking powder
1	cup cooked grits (page 12)
3	tablespoons melted butter or oil
2	tablespoons honey
1-2	eggs
1-1/2	cups buttermilk or plain yogurt
1	cup cheddar cheese, shredded

Preheat oven to 400°F.

Combine dry ingredients and optional spices in medium bowl. In blender or food processor, blend grits and liquid ingredients until creamy. Stir in cheese and optional ingredients.

Combine wet and dry mixtures. Do not overmix. Pour into a greased 8-inch baking pan.

Bake for 35-40 minutes. Cool on a wire rack.

Serves 8-12.

◆

Options:
Sliced
green chilies
jalapenos
sweet red peppers
minced onions

◆

◆ NO-KNEAD GRITS BREAD ◆

2	packages active dry yeast
2-1/2	cups warm water (105-115°F)
4	tablespoons honey
4	tablespoons butter or margarine
2	teaspoons salt
6	cups unbleached white flour
1	cup cooked grits (page 12)

In large bowl, dissolve yeast in water. Stir in honey. Add butter or margarine, salt, 4 cups flour and grits.

Beat on low speed with mixer until blended. Increase speed to high and beat for 1 minute. Scrape sides and beat 1 more minute. Stir in remaining flour with wooden spoon. Cover and let rise in warm place until doubled in bulk, about 45 minutes.

Grease 2 9x5-inch loaf pans. Punch batter down by stirring 30 strokes with a wooden spoon. Spoon into loaf pans. Cover and let rise in warm place for 30-40 minutes until batter rises to edge of pan (not over). Bake in preheated oven at 375°F for 35-40 minutes.

Remove from pan. (To test doneness, tap bottom of loaf. If it doesn't sound hollow, return to pan and bake 5 more minutes.) Cool on wire rack.

Makes 2 loaves.

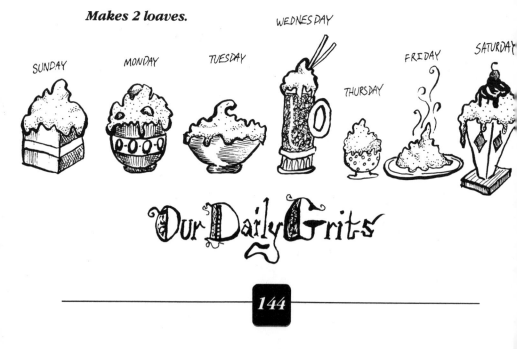

SUNDAY   MONDAY   TUESDAY   WEDNESDAY   THURSDAY   FRIDAY   SATURDAY

Our Daily Grits

*T**he following yeast recipes are tasty variations of no-knead bread. Grits provide a wonderfully spongy texture and your friends will think you spent all day kneading.***

♦ ♦ ♦ ♦

EASY CHEESE GRITS BREAD

2	packages active dry yeast
2-1/2	cups warm water (105-115°F)
4	tablespoons honey
4	tablespoons butter or margarine
2	teaspoons salt
6	cups unbleached white flour
1	cup cooked grits (page 12)
2	cups shredded cheddar cheese

In large bowl, dissolve yeast in water. Stir in honey. Add butter or margarine, salt, 4 cups flour and grits.

Beat on low speed with mixer until blended. Increase speed to high and beat for 1 minute. Scrape sides and beat 1 more minute. Stir in remaining flour and cheese with wooden spoon. Cover and let rise in warm place until doubled in bulk, about 45 minutes.

Grease 2 9x5-inch loaf pans. Punch batter down by stirring 30 strokes with a wooden spoon. Spoon into loaf pans. Cover and let rise in warm place for 30-40 minutes until batter rises to edge of pan (not over).

Bake in preheated oven at 375°F for 35-40 minutes.

Remove from pan. (To test doneness, tap bottom of loaf. If it doesn't sound hollow, return to pan and bake 5 more minutes.) Cool on wire rack.

Makes 2 loaves.

HANSEL & GRIT-EL GERMAN RYE BREAD

Grits clean up from your saucepans easier when cool. Just "peel" them out.

2	packages active dry yeast
2-1/2	cups warm water (105-115°F)
4	tablespoons honey
4	tablespoons butter or margarine
2	teaspoons salt
3	cups unbleached white flour
1	cup whole wheat flour
1	cup cooked grits (page 12)
2	cups rye flour
3	teaspoons caraway seeds

In large bowl, dissolve yeast in water. Stir in honey. Add butter or margarine, salt, 2 cups unbleached white flour, 1 cup whole wheat flour and grits.

Beat on low speed with mixer until blended. Increase speed to high and beat for 1 minute. Scrape sides and beat 1 more minute. Stir in remaining flour with wooden spoon. Cover and let rise in warm place until doubled in bulk, about 45 minutes.

Grease 2 9x5-inch loaf pans. Punch batter down by stirring 30 strokes with a wooden spoon, stirring in caraway seeds. Spoon into loaf pan. Cover and let rise in warm place for 30-40 minutes until batter rises to edge of pan (not over).

Bake in preheated oven at 375°F for 35-40 minutes.

Remove from pan. (To test doneness, tap bottom of loaf. If it doesn't sound hollow, return to pan and bake 5 more minutes.) Cool on wire rack.

Makes 2 loaves.

◆ CINNAMON RAISIN ◆ GRITS BREAD

2	packages active dry yeast
2-1/2	cups warm water (105-115°F)
4	tablespoons honey
4	tablespoons butter or margarine
2	teaspoons salt
3	cups unbleached white flour
3	cups whole wheat flour
1	cup cooked grits (page 12)
1	tablespoon cinnamon
2	cups raisins

Glaze:

1/2	cup powdered sugar
1	tablespoon milk
1/2	teaspoon vanilla

In large bowl, dissolve yeast in water. Stir in honey. Add butter or margarine, salt, 3 cups unbleached white flour, 1 cup whole wheat flour and grits.

Beat on low speed with mixer until blended. Increase speed to high and beat for 1 minute. Scrape sides and beat 1 more minute. Stir in remaining flour with wooden spoon. Cover and let rise in warm place until doubled in bulk, about 45 minutes.

Grease 2 9x5-inch loaf pans. Punch batter down by stirring 30 strokes with a wooden spoon. Swirl in cinnamon and raisins. Spoon into loaf pans. Cover and let rise in warm place for 30-40 minutes until batter rises to edge of pan (not over).

Bake in preheated oven at 375°F for 35-40 minutes. Remove from pan. (To test doneness, tap bottom of loaf. If it doesn't sound hollow, return to pan and bake 5 more minutes.) Cool on wire rack.

For glaze: Mix powdered sugar, milk and vanilla in measuring cup. Spread over cooled bread.

Makes 2 loaves.

◆ WHOLE WHEAT GRITS BREAD ◆

2	*packages active dry yeast*
2-1/2	*cups warm water (105-115°F)*
4	*tablespoons honey*
4	*tablespoons butter or margarine*
2	*teaspoons salt*
3	*cups unbleached white flour*
3	*cups whole wheat flour*
1	*cup cooked grits (page 12)*

In large bowl, dissolve yeast in water. Stir in honey. Add butter or margarine, salt, 2 cups unbleached white flour, 1 cup whole wheat flour and grits.

Beat on low speed with mixer until blended. Increase speed to high and beat for 1 minute. Scrape sides and beat 1 more minute. Stir in remaining flour with wooden spoon. Cover and let rise in warm place until doubled in bulk, about 45 minutes.

Grease 2 9x5-inch loaf pans. Punch batter down by stirring 30 strokes with a wooden spoon. Spoon into loaf pan. Cover and let rise in warm place for 30-40 minutes until batter rises to edge of pan (not over).

Bake in preheated oven at 375°F for 35-40 minutes.

Remove from pan. (To test doneness, tap bottom of loaf. If it doesn't sound hollow, return to pan and bake 5 more minutes.) Cool on wire rack.

Makes 2 loaves.

◆ CRISPY CORNMEAL ◆ YEAST BREAD

2	packages active dry yeast
2-1/2	cups warm water (105-115°F)
4	tablespoons honey
4	tablespoons butter or margarine
2	teaspoons salt
3	cups unbleached white flour
3	cups whole wheat flour
1	cup cooked grits (page 12)
1	cup yellow cornmeal

In large bowl, dissolve yeast in water. Stir in honey. Add butter or margarine, salt, 2 cups unbleached white flour, 1 cup whole wheat flour and grits.

Beat on low speed with mixer until blended. Increase speed to high and beat for 1 minute. Scrape sides and beat 1 more minute. Stir in remaining flour and cornmeal with wooden spoon. Cover and let rise in warm place until doubled in bulk, about 45 minutes.

Grease 2 9x5-inch loaf pans. Punch batter down by stirring 30 strokes with a wooden spoon. Spoon into loaf pan. Cover and let rise in warm place for 30-40 minutes until batter rises to edge of pan (not over).

Bake in preheated oven at 375° for 35-40 minutes.

Remove from pan. (To test doneness, tap bottom of loaf. If it doesn't sound hollow, return to pan and bake 5 more minutes.) Cool on wire rack.

Makes 2 loaves.

My sister-in-law Wendy created this wonderful bread machine recipe for me since I don't have one. She also lives in San Francisco which proves true grits lovers are everywhere!

WENDY'S WONDER GRITS BREAD
(For Bread Machines)

1-1/2   teaspoons yeast
1-1/2   cups bread flour
1   cup cooked grits (page 12)
2   teaspoons sugar
1/2   teaspoon salt
1   tablespoon margarine
2   tablespoons water

Place ingredients in order of appearance into your bread machine and follow instructions for your machine for a medium setting.

Makes one medium loaf.

GAIL'S BIS-GRITS

2	cups self-rising flour
1/2	teaspoon baking soda
1/4	cup butter or margarine
1	cup cooked grits (page 12)
3/4	cup plain yogurt or buttermilk

Preheat oven to 450°F. With a fork, stir together in large mixing bowl the flour and soda. Cut in butter or margarine using pastry blender, 2 knives or a fork. Blend until mixture resembles coarse crumbs.

In another bowl beat together grits and yogurt or buttermilk. Stir it into flour mixture, just until mixed. Transfer onto well-floured board and knead lightly (about 12 strokes). The dough will be sticky.

Roll out dough with rolling pin or pat out with hands to thickness of about 1/2-3/4 of an inch, depending on how big you like your biscuits. Cut with 2-inch biscuit cutter and place on ungreased baking sheet. Bake for about 10-12 minutes until lightly browned.

Healthy variation: Substitute 1 cup whole wheat and 1 cup unbleached white flour for self-rising flour. Add 2 teaspoons baking soda and 1 teaspoon salt in addition to the 1/2 teaspoon baking soda.

Makes 10 large or 12 smaller biscuits.

◆

After admitting my lack of biscuit expertise, my friend and editor Gail Poulton created these for me. She swears they're the best she's ever baked (and she doesn't usually swear).

◆

INDEX

D

E

M

P

NOTES

Titles available from Strawberry Patch:
Gone With The Grits
For Popcorn Lovers Only
The Pregnant Husband's Handbook
You Know You're A New Parent When...
1-800-875-7242